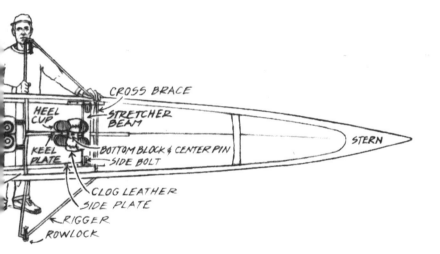

CROSS BRACE

STRETCHER BEAM

HEEL CUP

KEEL PLATE

BOTTOM BLOCK & CENTER PIN

SIDE BOLT

STERN

CLOG LEATHER

SIDE PLATE

RIGGER

ROWLOCK

THE SCULLER AT EASE

In memory of Bert Haines,
professional English sculler,
for many years coach of Harvard lightweight oarsmen.

THE SCULLER AT EASE

Frank Cunningham

and

Leslie Stillwell Strom

Illustrations by Laurie Cunningham

Revised edition
First published in hardcover edition by Avery Press, 1992.

copyright © 1999, 1992 by Frank Cunningham
Illustrations copyright © 1999, 1992 Laurie Cunningham

Printed in the United States of America
All rights reserved.

ISBN 0-9674651-0-9

Grandview Street Press
PMB 121, 4509 Interlake Avenue N.
Seattle, WA 98103
USA

Library of Congress Card Number: pending

Cover layout by avenue B design, Seattle
Book design by Laurie Cunningham
Page Layout by Carlos Palacian
Printing by Universal Printing, Seattle

ACKNOWLEDGEMENTS

to Christopher Cunningham for taking the manuscript in hand
when it came time to ready it for publication;
to Stan Pocock for his continued support of what is best in the
heritage handed down to us by the Thames watermen;
to Charley McIntyre for his keen eye and unflagging support
on and off the water;
to Hartley Rogers for his thoughtful and charitable criticism of
the initial faltering manuscript;
to Tom Mendenhall for his many kindnesses and encouragement
before the book took form and afterward;
and to Harry and Betty Stanton, Austin Olney, and Marcia Legru
for their heroic efforts to secure a publisher for the book.

and to a line of scullers and rowers
stretching backward to 1948 whose enthusiasm,
even passion for the sport,
has been the delight of my life.

TABLE OF CONTENTS

INTRODUCTION

I f you want to learn to scull on your own, you will have to place more reliance on what you feel and what you hear while you are in a boat, than on what you see. Set about it as if you were blind; you will learn faster if you trust your senses rather than your intellect.

The world of the sculler is topsy-turvy: forward is backward, right is left, up is down. You must sit backward to do your work through a fulcrum. Because your eyes dominate the direction of your ordinary movements, vision can get in the way when you try to depend on it in the unfamiliar territory of a sculling boat. It interferes with the signals coming from your hands and your ears.

To learn trust in your other senses, find a wherry or similar wide, safe boat that will allow you to experience all the characteristics of a racing shell except its extreme instability. You can then respond to the feel of the boat under you and the sculls in your hands, without the apprehension that a mistake will cost you a capsize. At first you may be inclined to be careful and deliberate, but as you become more confident you will be able to take the small risks without which you cannot achieve mastery.

To learn the quickness and spontaneity that characterize good sculling, spend some time watching animals. From them you can learn the grace that comes from their economy of movement and their complete reliance on their senses.

Be patient. Do not try to force your will on the boat, the sculls or the water. Let them teach you. Become as simple as a child. Be at ease with yourself and you will be at ease in your boat.

✦ FUNDAMENTALS ✦
PREPARING TO ROW

THINGS TO LEARN BEFORE GETTING INTO A BOAT

As a rule, boats with sliding seats are not the best ones to learn to scull in. Apprehension about making mistakes, running into something, even rolling over, will work very strongly against the acquisition of sound technique, even in a forgiving boat like a wherry. So, even before you get into such a boat you should learn how sculls work.

THE WAY THE SCULLS WORK

The best way to learn how the blade works is with your hand in the water. When your hand and arm are kept in line and rotated about their central axis, you have an oar of sorts; however, this oar feels everything that is done to it. It will be necessary, of course, if you are to imitate the working of an oar properly, to get your elbow wet. Keeping the hand and arm completely immersed, pass your arm back and forth, pushing the water with the palm of your hand, slipping back through the water with the hand rotated thumb first to prepare for the next stroke.

Keep your "oar" underwater as it moves back and forth just by letting your hand take whatever angle it must to bring this about. Observe what is going on, and discover the secret of the oar for yourself. I'll suppose that you have brought this book down to the boathouse float—or to the bathtub—and, having done some experimenting, are prepared to compare notes.

♦ At the beginning of the stroke did you begin pressing your palm against the water before it was vertical?

♦ Before you began the return or recovery, did you start to turn your hand?

♦ Did you consciously plan to make either of these gestures? Or did they just happen?

Watch fish in a tank moving their pectoral fins. The action of these fins is very much like rowing or paddling.

Obviously, an oar used in the conventional way must leave the water. But let's find out whether it is necessary to put it in the water and take it out again with a sharp vertical motion. Or whether it is possible to slip it in and out again without a vertical movement at either end of the stroke.

Put your hand and arm back in the water and repeat the experiment. Then, gradually raise your hand until the recovery, or return half of the stroke, takes place with your hand skimming the surface. On the pull-through the water will come only halfway up your hand. You can now "row" with no upward or downward movement whatsoever.

It is only a short step to row with your hand fully covered by the water, and clear the water on the backward pass. But now your hand leaves the water at an angle and rises diagonally, pushing aside a small amount of water as it goes. You may think that this interference is an obstacle. And it would be, were it not for the fact that a well-pulled oar creates turbulence in the water behind it. This turbulence offers little resistance to the blade.

The essence of a good catch is lightning quickness. With your hand resting lightly on the water, start the swing of your arm as quickly as possible. Pretend you are Bruce Lee in "Fists of Fury". Rotate your hand as your arm starts to move, but reactively. You will be able to send a sheet of water ahead of your half-covered hand. (Don't forget to close the shower curtain.) The object is to find out how quickly you can shear the water and send it flying.

You will perceive quickness as pressure on the palm of your hand. The quicker the movement, the quicker the buildup of pressure. (Later, with a scull or an oar in your fingers, you will feel this buildup of pressure in the hook of your fingers.) Continue to drive the water ahead of your hand, gradually immersing it until no water breaks away from your palm. In other words, cover your hand as quickly as possible.

So, it is perfectly possible to learn a great deal about rowing, and to learn it intuitively, before entering a boat. When you pick up a scull you should think of the blade as the palm of your hand. Feel everything that is happening to the blade. Feel the pressure of the water on either side of it, and respond. Don't think; just react. Trust your senses.

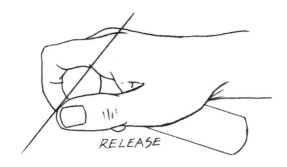

RELEASE

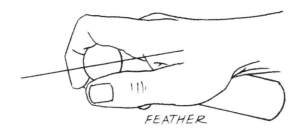

FEATHER

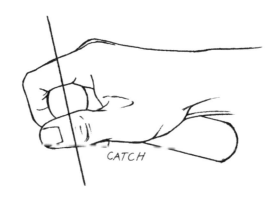

CATCH

THE HOLD
In rowing it is your hand that first responds to your fears. Apprehension inevitably tightens your hand. Begin to develop sure hands by practising the hold on a dowel. Teachers of the violin often introduce the proper hold of a bow with exercises using a pencil, which is lighter and less unwieldy than the real thing. The dowel will enable your fingers to become as familiar with the scull handle as the basketball player who spends hours handling the ball.

A dowel of an inch and five-eighths in diameter, about a foot long would be appropriate. The dowel must offer a suitable area for the fingers to rest comfortably upon, and be long enough to project a good hand's breadth beyond your grip. It must be slightly rounded at one end, but only enough to soften the edges.

A line drawn across the end of the dowel will allow you to gauge its rotation as you practise turning it with your fingers. Take the dowel in your hand as shown in the illustration. Notice that it lies at an angle to your hand. Notice too that the hand and arm lie in a line. The thumb touches but does not grip the end of the dowel. The dowel will project beyond your hand so that you can hold it in position with your other hand.

Draw the handle under your hand by curling your fingers, thus rotating it. Allow it to pass across your thumb. It should still make an angle with your hand. If your hand makes a right angle to the dowel then you have turned your wrist laterally, adding, rather than easing, tension in your arm. And worse, you will have lost the quickness that the proper hold will give you.

Rotate the handle in the opposite direction by flexing your fingers at the first joint of your hand (at the base of your fingers), allowing it to pass again across your thumb. Continue to make this gesture until it seems natural and easy. Then, switch hands.

Notice that the line you have drawn across the end of the dowel has rotated about 70 degrees. Don't be concerned if you can't turn it the 90 degrees that a scull turns from feather to catch. Water pressure on the face of the blade will force it against the upright portion of the rowlock. In time you may learn to kick the handle around with the tips of your fingers rather than by squeezing it. In a boat you will learn to begin your stroke with a strong push against the stretcher. Your fingers will respond spontaneously to the shove of your legs, and quick as a blink, your blade is in the water, solidly hooked.

The renowned violinist Yehudi Menuhin has said, *"The violinist's enemy is any tightness of hold..."*[1] The same applies to the sculler. A light sure hold is the key to good sculling. It spells the difference between ease and confidence—at any stroke rate—and rapidly tiring, tense, and injured forearms and wrists.

POSTURE

In *The Snow People²*, Marie Herbert describes her experiences among Eskimos of the west coast of Greenland. *"I could not help noticing how straight their backs were whenever they bent over. They seemed to bend from the hips 'chevron shaped'..."*

Unquestionably, they know the best way to protect their backs from fatigue and muscle spasms. In the same way, you should protect your back by lengthening it from your hips to make the catch, that is, the beginning of the stroke.

The easiest way to learn the rotation of the hips that produces the elongated back is to sit on the edge of a chair and alternately slump and sit up, moving your lower back through the greatest range possible. There are a few muscles that will have to be stretched out to allow this movement to take place in a boat. So, sit on the floor, legs extended and separated a foot or so, and repeat the movements already described. Eventually, the stretching of your hamstrings will have greatly improved your effective reach.

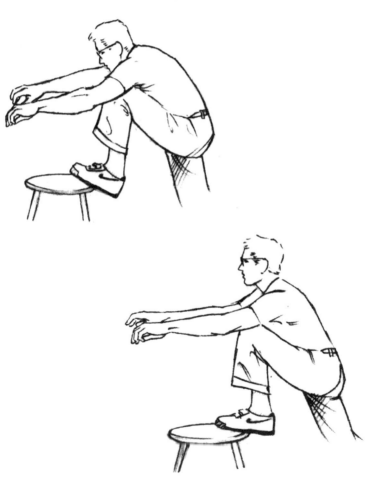

BALANCE

"The violinist must develop a feeling in body, limbs and fingers of exquisite and precise balance..." —Yehudi Menuhin

Like sitting in a kayak or on a rolling log, keeping your weight under control in a sculling boat brings into play the small muscles of the torso. If the large mass of the torso can be kept centered above the boat by the delicate and immediate play of these small muscles, the business of achieving a light but sure hold on the oar or sculls is greatly simplified. Nearly everybody has a sufficient sense of balance to scull. No special training is necessary.

Do smaller people, say, 5'–2", 115 pounds, have as much difficulty balancing a boat as large people 6'–6", 220 pounds? Almost never. This is because the weight of a smaller person is concentrated nearer the boat's center of rotation.

However, sitting in any racing shell is going to make you a bit uneasy at first. But if you keep your blades on the water and your hands in about the same plane, the boat will be quite stable. It then becomes a good deal easier to manage than a bicycle. Apprehension fades, and your balance will improve as you gain confidence.

THE ROWING ENVIRONMENT

WATER AND WEATHER

The first observation every good waterman makes is the size and direction of surface waves, not only near at hand, but as far as he can see on the course he intends to take. Look for alternative courses that take advantage of protected water in the lee of land masses, large buildings, ships at moorings or docks. On any body of water, wind and wave conditions vary from side to side, from end to end.

"The wind came up."
You will hear that from the sculler who returns to the boathouse after a harrowing passage. The old hand knows that it is no excuse. "Yes, it almost always does at this time of day when the wind is in that quarter." Develop a nose for weather and and an eye for the protected shore. Know where the sheltered water is and head for it.

Be aware that where the wind blows onto a bulkhead or wall rising from the water, waves bounce back to create steeper cresting waves that easily overwhelm a small boat. It is always safer to go with a partner if you are in a single scull.

TRAFFIC
It is easy to get into trouble on the water in any kind of boat, easier still in a racing shell. Study the traffic patterns on the water you plan to use. Commercial boats observe rules of the road, carry appropriate lights and look where they are going. The basso profundo of their large powerful engines is more easily felt than heard. Sometimes commercial vessels draw large wakes. Tugboats tow barges and rafts. Stay out of their way. Pleasure boats are a lot less predictable. Avoid them. Although legally you have the right of way, develop an eye for course and speed and set your course to put the greatest distance between them and you.

Channel buoys define the pathway of deeper water, red to one side, green to the other. Navigation markers may not be lighted or, for that matter, very visible from your low vantage point. Whenever you can, leave these marked lanes for the vessels that need them, and skirt the outside. The water that is too shallow for these large boats is deep enough for the boat you are in.

If you must row on a busy waterway keep to the right side of the channel.

GETTING USED TO A BOAT

CARRYING A BOAT

Two people can carry a single or a double from a point three feet or so from each end, right side up, upside down or on its side, so long as it rests in the crook of the arm. Wooden boats are easily damaged when rowers carry them too close to the ends and, without thinking, squeeze them. Fiberglass boats are less vulnerable. Watch the riggers going out the door and, because they are wide, be careful to set them in the water well clear of the dock. Remember also that these boats are very long and don't go around corners well! Carry wherries right side up from the ends with your hand under the keel.

PUTTING SCULLS IN THE ROWLOCKS

Put the dockside scull into its rowlock first, and secure the gate. Draw the scull through the rowlock until the collar makes contact. Then, insert the waterside scull in its rowlock. Tall people can crouch in the center of the boat on one leg and easily reach the waterside rowlock to close its gate. Short people will have to lie across the boat, a little uncomfortable, but safe. After the waterside scull is in place and the gate secured, draw it across the boat, so that wind and wave don't swing it around and make the handle hard to reach.

GETTING INTO AND STABILIZING THE BOAT
When you get into a boat, every movement seems somehow to be reversed. You face backward rather than forward, and this may lead to disorientation. Bring someone with you on your first attempt.

Having made sure that the sculls are in the rowlocks and the gates closed and tight, face aft and pick up the handles with your waterside hand, and butt the ends together. The collars should be snug in the rowlocks and the handles located over your heel cups.

Place your dockside hand on the gunwale near the aft end of the tracks, or around the rigger if it joins the boat at this point. With your weight on your dockside leg, use the waterside foot to roll the seat bow-ward and immediately place that foot on the centerline of the rower's platform at the stern end of the tracks. The seat should roll back to nudge your heel.

Before you transfer your weight to the boat, make sure the rigger will not touch the dock and be forced upward. Your dockside foot will now rest lightly on the dock.

Next, bring that foot into the boat, extend it straight out in front of you and sit down. You need not, should not, move either hand. If you prefer, you may place the dockside foot on the track next to the other foot and let your weight into the seat with both legs.

Not until you are safely in your seat should you try to get your feet into the clogs or shoes. Remember, you are getting into a boat, not trying on a pair of shoes.

GETTING OUT OF THE BOAT
Before you leave the dock, practise getting out of the boat. Leave the boat in reverse order, taking the same care not to allow the rigger to bear against the dock.

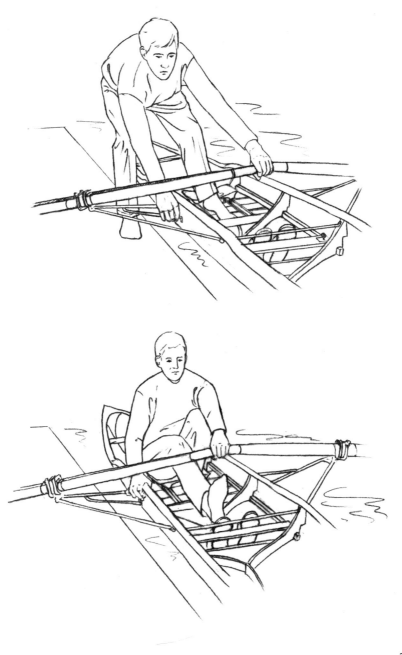

First, butt the scull handles together with your waterside hand loosely wrapped around them. Next, slip your waterside foot out of the clog or shoe and place it in the center of the rower's bench about even with the rowlocks.

Place your dockside hand loosely around the part of the rigger nearest you, close to the boat. Rock forward on the waterside leg, pulling yourself up to the handles. Use the dockside hand to stabilize and center your body on its way up. (If necessary, bring the other foot up and place it on the track beside the first foot.) Stand up. If you have made no move toward the dock, the boat will remain exactly in place beside it. Reach out your dockside foot and place it on the dock *outside* the rigger. *Do not lunge toward the dock.* This will push your boat away! Transfer your weight to the dockside foot. Bring your other foot to the dock and draw the waterside oar across the boat.

In both maneuvers the blades must be bearing gently on water and dock, so your handles must be pulled upward. At the first sign of instability most people drop the handles, worsening things considerably. It takes a while to become accustomed to reacting in the opposite way from what is familiar on dry land. There are, of course, other ways of entering and leaving a boat, but none is as likely to protect the boat and to ensure the rower against embarrassment. Setting a foot temporarily on the keelson while loosening a shoe or clog can be dangerous to the fragile skin of a wooden boat. Placing hands on the coamings has accounted for most of the damage to them.

Wipe your boat off before you put it away. Keeping boats clean and dry minimizes rot in wooden boats and removes a residue of oil or other organic matter that is potentially harmful to fiberglass. While wiping down your boat, look for damage, cracks, and other problems which may require attention.

GETTING AWAY FROM THE DOCK
When you are ready to depart, be sure the collars are snug against the rowlocks. The waterside blade should be resting on the water curving upward; the dockside blade should be resting on the dock face down. Keeping light upward pressure on the handles with your waterside hand, push away from the dock with the heel of your hand. Lean slightly on the waterside blade to let the other blade traverse the surface of the dock with a minimum of friction. Wait until the boat stops moving sideways.

You will not have moved far enough to clear the dock with that blade, so now start backing the stern into the dock with the waterside blade, even allowing the stern to make light contact with it. Then, continue to back with that blade until you can reach out your dockside hand, and take the blade clear of the dock. Row the boat away.

There is, of course, a lubberly way to do this, unthinkable in the days of wooden oars. That is to overhaul the dockside scull across the boat, pulling it through the rowlock until you can push the end of the blade against the dock. You will probably break off the tip of a wooden blade, since the grain runs out of the wood at this part of it. An oar isn't a setting pole, and oughtn't to be used like one in the first place.

ADJUSTING THE STRETCHER

If the shoes or clogs are ready to receive your feet, slip your feet in them. If they are not, place your feet on top of them and take a few short strokes away from the dock. You might as well get used to making adjustments to the stretcher when you are away from the dock. Dock space is frequently insufficient for the number of rowers who want to use it at a given time, so courtesy requires that you spend as little time as possible getting away.

After you are clear of the dock and other boats, prepare to adjust your stretcher and lace up your clogs or shoes by bringing both handles to your waist and leaning over them to secure them. Place your feet over the side of the boat. (Don't drop your heels in the water!)

Set the stretcher beam at a position that permits you to carry your handles just clear of your body as you complete the stroke. If the beam is too far sternward, your handles will strike your body at the finish of the stroke. If it is too far forward—toward the bow—you will be forced to finish the stroke awkwardly, depending too much on your arms rather than your shoulders and back.

When you have tightened the stretcher beam, lace yourself loosely in your shoes or clogs.

ON THE WATER AT LAST
LEARNING SCULLING ON THE FIXED SLIDE

Fixed-slide rowing has great value. It restricts your swing to the segment that provides the greatest stability. It teaches the value of using your weight to move the boat, to the very end of the stroke. It develops the habit of elongating, rather than hooping your back, to maximize reach. It encourages you to start the stroke with the arms loose and well-extended, countering a tendency to "muscle" the oar with your arms. It invites you to use your shoulders to keep the blade working as long as possible. Do lots of fixed-slide rowing. It builds confidence and it lays a good foundation for rowing on the moving slide.

STABILIZING THE BOAT

Once clear of the dock, lay your blades flat on the water with the tips curving upward, sit with your knees down, and alternately raise and lower the handles a few times to get the response of the boat. Then, keeping one blade still, scrub the other back and forth on the water, tipping the leading edge up each time to keep the blade from catching the water.

Hold your opposite hand lower to allow the working hand to pass over it unobstructed and, together with a slight shift of weight to that side, to provide stability to the boat. The tipping of the blade at each change of direction must become automatic. With the blade in constant touch with the water, your hand will sense what the blade is doing and react.

Keep playing with the blades until each hand responds correctly every time. Remember, a light touch on the handle guarantees complete control.

HOLDING THE SCULL

With the blades horizontal, the flat of the sleeves resting on the sill of the rowlock, settle your hands on the grips as you did with the dowel. Your forefingers will rest on the radiused end of the handle and the second joint of the second finger will be approximately at the top of it. The pads of the thumbs will touch the lower corner of the handle just opposite the forefingers. The illustration shows how this hold partly conceals the end of the handle.

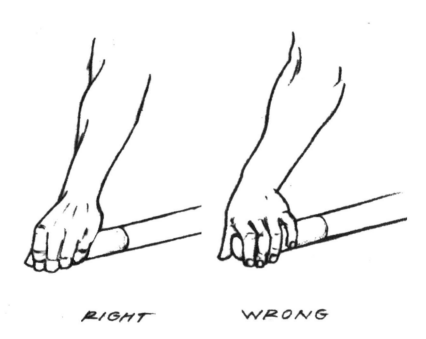

RIGHT   WRONG

THE SCULLER'S CATCH

At the zoo one day I stood awhile watching orangutans moving about in a desultory way, filling the time, as it were, swinging their arms and deciding whether or not to commit themselves to some small exertion or other. Their movements, then, were nearly unpredictable, so when they committed themselves to a convenient branch, the resultant swinging flight was magically abrupt. I watched their hands to see how they anticipated their holds, and discovered that the opening and closing of their fingers was so casual as to suggest that the fingers were operating independently of their owners. And, of course, they were executing the perfect sculler's catch, hooking the branches with their fingers!

But why should an orangutan be able to execute the catch better than most rowers and scullers? There are, I believe, two reasons. One is that the orangutan's thumb is placed differently on its hand, lower, one might say, and out of the way. The second is that its thumbs are not completely opposable. When we bring the thumb into play either under the handle or across the end of it, a familiar reflex is called into play and the thumb closes on and grasps the handle. An orangutan wouldn't do this. Swinging from tree branches requires that the hand be used like a hook. To grasp the branch with the thumb would result in serious damage to the inside of the thumb and the palm of the hand. The form of an orangutan's hand is a perfectly shaped device for insuring the survival of a species of animal that lives in trees.

So, in order to manage an oar or scull properly, we have paradoxically to turn back the evolutionary clock and learn to use our hands as if we did not possess opposable thumbs.

It is usual to think that the blade ought to be turned at right angles to the water before it enters. But, since the essence of a good catch is quickness, the best way to acquire quickness is to ignore ordinary logic and rely on reflex. Begin by settling the boat to one side, lowering that hand and shifting a little of your weight to that blade to do so. Keep the handle down on your thigh close to your waist. In this way you will be able to take the opposite blade out of the water without over-balancing the boat.

Without moving your seat, reach out, sliding the free blade along the surface of the water. When you reach the limit of your forward swing, pause, and fling yourself bowward. Do this in the expectation that your fingers will automatically turn the handle. You will be putting what you learned with the dowel to the test!

But suppose the blade crabs or flies across the water. You may be tempted to make your next attempt very cautiously, or to use your wrist. Don't! Remember your experiments in the bathtub and use only your fingers to turn the scull, *after* you have flung yourself bowward, not *before*.

This is the only way you are going to be able to "surprise" your fingers and train them to respond instantly to pressure on the face of the blade. It is the surest and quickest way to learn to cover the blade with the lightning quickness that is at the heart of good rowing.

I was trying to explain the catch in answer to a query I got in the mail, and while searching for an analogy, I hit on the way a duck's foot reacts to the forward and backward motion of its legs. The flaring and closing of the toes does not occur as a result of a conscious effort—I can't bring myself to believe that it does—so it happens because something else brings it about, a reflex in response to the water pressure on the surface of the foot, perhaps. All ducks are born with that reflex; without it I can't imagine how they would be able to swim. A duck's "catch" works very nicely, not a moment too soon, not a moment too late. There is an easy way to distinguish a well-made catch: listen to it. There should be little or no sound of broken water. Breaking, disturbed water signals the loss of energy. The quieter, the better.

THE PULL-THROUGH

The draw of the stroke takes the handles from the catch to the release. It is most effective when you throw your weight away from the handles and just hang on. Beginners want to pull the handles toward themselves with their arms, so their efforts have a tentative look. As your confidence grows, it becomes easier for you to leave the arms at full stretch and swing your back away from the stretcher. In this way you can add your weight to the strength of your muscles and considerably increase your pulling power.

Think of the pull-through as continuing past the release. In other words, follow through in the same way a golfer or a batter swings through the ball. This will bring you quickly into position for the next stroke and keep the boat moving forward. The effectiveness of your stroke depends on keeping the blade well covered. Listen for the sound of water breaking against your blades that tells you that your blades are slipping and not properly anchored.

HAND CROSSOVER

I don't know how many times I have encountered scullers, both men and women, for whom scraped knuckles are a chronic condition. They may have sculled for years, yet the problem persists. They may get through the major part of the day's outing unscathed, but sooner or later, their hands collide and blood flows. Proof again that two objects cannot occupy the same space at the same time.

To maximize leverage, scull handles extend past the centerline of the boat, overlapping. Some arrangements have to be made so that you can take advantage of the leverage gained in this way without rolling the boat or barking your knuckles. One way is to raise one rigger higher than the other. This will allow you to pass one hand directly over the other at mid-stroke. A less drastic way is to rig at nearly even heights, and to maintain the balance of the boat by drawing one hand *ahead* of the other on the pull-through and sending one hand *away* before the other on the return.

Assuming that your boat is rigged nearly flat, that is, with the starboard rigger 1/4 to 1/2 inch higher than port (according to the American convention), you will be sculling left hand over right. As you extend your arms for the catch, reach out a little farther with your left. (Imagine your left arm is longer than your right.) As you pull through keep your boat level by pulling your right hand ahead of your left. Allow your left wrist to arch to accommodate your right hand under it. As you continue to pull through, allow both wrists to arch and remain arched through the remainder of the stroke. At the very end of the stroke, your wrists will come down slightly, as you turn the blade to release it.

To cross over during the recovery, send your right hand away ahead of your left to allow your left hand and handle to settle onto your right wrist. When your hands begin to separate, move your left hand out beyond your right to make ready for the catch. The alternativeway to return your handles is to send your left hand away before your right, but you will have to arch your left wrist quickly to accommodate your right hand under it.

THE RELEASE

A good release looks easy—is easy—because there are forces acting on the oar or scull that will do most of the work for you. We pull on our sculls with our fingers wrapped over the tops of the handles, our fists pronated, imparting rotation to the scull. For this reason the rowlock is inclined slightly to counter this rotation. The resistance exerted on the scull by the rowlock is, therefore, greatest near the upper edge of the sleeve. As you complete the stroke there is an instant when you can pivot your sculls on this upper edge, just by tipping your wrists downward a very small amount.

Firm your wrists so that you can send the handles away and start the blades forward. If you aim your handles a bit below the horizontal, your blades will rise diagonally out of the water heading toward the bow. As your blades leave the water, relax your fingers to allow your sculls to settle in the rowlocks and your blades will be "on the feather," clear of the water. Since the arcs traced by your sculls are taking your handles away from the centerline of the boat, press your scull collars firmly against the rowlocks as you complete the stroke to achieve a good release. When you have released your blades properly, you will see very little broken, white water around the puddles. You will also come to know the sound of a good release.

To let your wrists drop under the handles is fatal to a clean release. Your blades have already turned enough to maintain a solid grip of the water and are ready to slip out when your handles are struck away. As the blades leave the water, your fingers allow the handles to roll, laying the sculls on the feather. The best way to ensure a perfect release is to feel the handles trying to pull themselves out of your hands as you change direction. A proper release will eliminate trapping your blades in the water, washing out your finish, striking your thighs with your wrists on the recovery and depressing the bow of the boat.

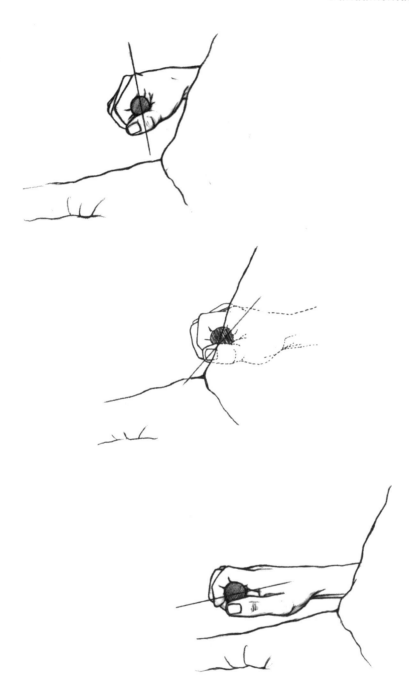

SCULLING ON THE MOVING SLIDE

Start rowing with the bow-most quarter of the slide. Later, you can use more and more. Reach from your hips rather than from the middle of your back, keep your head up, and continue to row as you did without the slide.

As you learn to extend the stroke by using more and more of your slide, think of *increasing* the distance from your hips to the handle as you approach the catch. As you use more slide it becomes harder and harder to reach out farther without bending your back. Bending your back shortens this distance. If you think of squeezing an orange between your torso and your thighs, you can gradually acquire the ability to take the curve out of your lower back and to reach without strain.

Every catch should be made with the seat behind you rather than under you. To force a reach by bending your back takes you past your "strong point," as Steve Fairbairn[3] called it, that is, the point at which the back is stacked up on itself, firm and unyielding. *A bent back bends.* When you throw all your weight on the handle at the instant of the catch, energy that should go out to the oar has to be used to counter the increasing bend in your back. With your back properly positioned, all the power of your legs goes directly to your handles.

Use the full range of your shoulders to bring your handles in. Imagine that a wire is strung between your shoulders when you are at the catch. It will lie several inches away from your collar bones. As you approach the finish your shoulders should draw back and cause the wire to cut through your collarbones (A bit grisly to contemplate!). If, as you finish the stroke, the wire still crosses in front of your shoulders, you are not using your shoulders properly. It is the final movement of the shoulders, *not the arms*, that brings the handles home. Failure to use your shoulders permits your elbows to rise as you complete the stroke. If this happens the load falls on your arms, the weakest link. It is this working of the shoulders that permits you to keep pressure on the handles while at the same time start moving the rest of your body out of the bow.

Failure to use your shoulders properly results in finishing your stroke too soon. You find yourself in the bow of the boat and your blades out of the water. You must make a separate effort to start your body sternward.

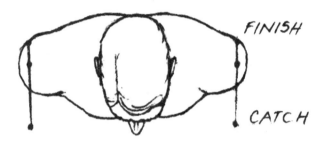

THE RHYTHM OF THE SLIDE

If you pull through properly, your slide will move rapidly at first; then, as your legs straighten, it will slow down and stop. It should not move again until you have swung your body back through the upright position, so press hard with your legs as you finish the stroke. Keep your seat pressed firmly into the bow while you pivot your body from the hips.

Continue to swing your body until your hands pass over your knees. Assume the catch position as you pass half slide. Continue to move toward the stern, making no effort to slow down until you are within an inch or so of the front stops. Take more time traversing that inch than you did getting to it.

You may feel at first as though this rapid initial movement of your body is producing a "fast slide." That is because swinging your body through the entire arc from finish to catch creates that feeling. In reality, your slide will move quite deliberately.

POSTURE AGAIN

Watch people get into chairs. Chances are that when their weight settles into the seat, their lower backs are rounded in a slump and their weight carried over their tailbones. Look at the lower six or eight inches of the back. At what angle does it come off the seat? Perpendicular? Angled forward? Backward?

Watch a concert pianist sit down to play. What does his or her back look like? Have you ever seen one play from a slouch? How about an equestrian? Straight back, leaning slightly forward from the hips, what is called "a good seat." Very important in riding, both for the rider and the mount. The rider is comfortable, relaxed, in control of the horse. The horse is spared the repeated shocks of the rider's weight.

What the pianist and the equestrian know—from instinct or training, but I strongly suspect training—is that unless their spines are in perfect alignment, they cannot possibly produce good performances. In a sport like rowing it is especially important to align the spine properly to minimize the possibility of back strain or injury at the outset. Too many in the sport are ready to concede that injuries to the back are, if not inevitable, probable.

The first thing to do upon entering a boat is to "walk" your buttocks towards the bow, to settle your weight nearer your thighs and draw the curve out of your lower back. Some people do this spontaneously, but usually it is because they have had training in a musical instrument, or typing, or dance, or—as in days gone by—they have been taught drawing-room manners, including, of course, how to sit. Seated in this way, your back is properly aligned to prevent fatigue. Reach from the hips, eliminating altogether the need to try to reach from the middle of the back.

> To Summarize:
> *You must protect your back throughout the stroke. Yet your back must transmit all the power of the legs directly—without yielding—to the blade. So, with your back elongated, relatively straight, your lower back pressed down, and your head up, your spinal column is in position and ready to work hard.*

LEG DRIVE

It helps to think of a bit of string tied between the seat and the handle as you sit at the catch. At the catch the string is taut. "Shooting the slide," that is, allowing the legs to drive the seat out from under your body, will break the string. Conversely, surging upward with the back will cause the string to go slack. Think, then, of keeping the string taut for about two-thirds of the leg drive.

In the boat there is one dramatic proof of a well-begun stroke, especially from a dead start: You will rise off your seat.

The whole weight of your body, suspended between the handles and the stretcher, will rise off the seat. At that moment you will understand perfectly what is meant by "good coupling." As you become more skillful with your blades, you can abandon yourself to the simple joy of bending the oar in the first millisecond, so throw caution to the wind; explode off the stretcher. There is, of course, the problem of the seat rolling sternward while you are poised in mid-air. It will be gone when you return. Years ago oarsmen used to apply shellac to the seats of their trunks to keep their seats under them. However, a judicious and subtle adjustment of the way you take the beginning will keep your seat under control with no loss of power.

You may wonder what lifting your body off the seat does to the boat. Good bladework and an instantaneous catch *prevent* the boat from moving backward an unacceptable amount.

PULL-THROUGH

To keep a constant pressure on your blades you have to counter the force of your leg drive by keeping all your weight applied to moving the handles until after you change direction with your body. Your arms will begin to bend as the boat speeds up, but it is best not to think of using your arms to finish the stroke. Instead, use your shoulders to "reel in" the handle. All the parts of your body, working in unison, will produce a perfectly coordinated stroke. The seat, the hands, and the back will complete their motion at virtually the same instant. The pull-through is not produced by a succession of separate efforts by the legs, the back and the arms but by all working together. You can get a clearer sense of what the pull-through ought to look like by watching animals leaping. You should feel the well-drawn stroke as a single surge of energy.

THE RECOVERY

The object of the recovery is twofold: to return to the beginning of the stroke as quickly as possible, and to maximize the run of the boat. It begins before the blades come out of the water. This is the moment when you have to be able to do two things at once. At the completion of the drive press your legs down and use the weight of your body to finish the stroke. An instant before your handles arrive at the end of the stroke, start your body, head first, out of the bow, meanwhile keeping full pressure on the blades with your shoulders. Make the change of direction without the least appearance of "chinning" yourself on your handles. Keep pressure on your handles with your shoulders. Keep your feet pressed into the stretcher. You will be able to release the blades cleanly and easily *while* your sculls are bent. Any slackening of effort, any pressure whatsoever against the tops of your feet, tells you that the bend is coming out of your sculls, that they are about to be trapped by the water.

Carry your weight to the stern as rapidly as you can, rotating your hips, until you have positioned your seat behind you and straightened your lower back. You will have assumed the position you need to begin the stroke as you pass through half slide. As you traverse the last inch of slide, take time to rest, relax and ready yourself for the next stroke while you let the boat run. Without any further movement of torso or arms, time your catch to coincide with your arrival at the front stops. If you are well-compressed at the hips, "squeezing the orange," you won't hit them.

STROKE RATE AND PROPORTION

Stroke rate is sometimes a gauge of speed, sometimes a gauge of effort, or sometimes a gauge of progress down a race course. It is possible to row at a high rate and make poor speed, and just as possible to row at a low rate and make good speed. Place more importance on the speed of the boat than on any desire to row a high rate. To move a boat efficiently the ratio between the time the blade is in the water and the time it is in the air has to be very finely controlled. If too little time is allowed for the boat to run between shoves of the blade, the boat will check, or hesitate. If too much time is allowed the speed will fall off too far and your work will have been done in vain. Let economy of effort be your guide. Row a fixed distance at varying stroke rates to discover which one produces the best time. Experience tells us that the ratio of stroke to recovery will be between 1:1 and 1:1–1/2 at racing rates, longer on the paddle.

You will do a large part of your rowing at less than racing rates, developing a sense of the run of the boat. Learn ratio and slide control by extending the time on the slide so that you can keep the slide moving at ratios of 1:3, 1:4, or even 1:5. Stroke rate, then, is meaningless unless it is qualified by efficient rowing. You sometimes hear people say that a certain crew would have gone faster if they had raised the rate. It is more likely that the crew would have gone faster if they had rowed better, if they had been more meticulous about their bladework.

WATERMANSHIP

THE EVERYDAY SKILLS OF BOAT HANDLING

BACKING

Ayoung friend was telling me about her stay at a well-known sculling camp. "Backing," she said, "is not taught there." Backing a boat had no place in the curriculum, yet it must be obvious that the easiest and safest way for a beginner to learn to steer a boat is to go backward, so he can see where he's going. Skillful management of a racing shell backwards as well as forwards is essential to a competitor.

To prepare to back, lay your blades on the water, feathered, and slip your hands over the handles until the first joints of your fingers lie on top. Rock your wrists downward until your blades are at a 45 degree angle to the water, and push your handles away.

To make successive backing strokes, start to roll the blade, to lessen its "angle of attack" a little before you take it from the water. As you discovered in the bathtub experiment, this is the easiest way to achieve the "recovery." There is no need to lift the blade out of the water. Just slide it back across the water with a light hold, keeping what is now the leading edge of the blade tilted up to prevent crabbing. Backing in this fashion eliminates the problem of balancing the boat that is created when you lift the blades from the water. The vertical movement of the handles and blades is kept to a minimum. Best of all, you will learn to have absolute confidence in the sure, quick reflexes in your hands. And you will begin to sense what swimming and paddling are like for creatures that are born knowing.

STOPPING A BOAT

Scullers, and rowers in all "blind" (uncoxed) boats must

take a keen interest in learning to stop a boat quickly. The essence of a quick, controlled stop is to apply resistance equally on both sides of the boat. One marginally effective way to do this is to push upward on the handles, forcing the backs of the blades hard against the water. But a better way is to lay the feathered blades against the water, shift the hands slightly over the handles as if you were going to take a backing stroke, and then tip the leading edges just enough to allow them to enter the water. With a firm grip, guide your blades downward until the looms are covered for perhaps two feet. Hold on until it is practicable to roll the faces of your blades against the water. With a little practise you can do this confidently and safely.

Sad to say, we don't see many scullers or rowers able to do this now. In the long history of rowing it was, however, the standard method, much better adapted to maintaining a stable boat, and direction. It depends less on hope, and more on good management of the oar. When there is no time to lose, when an emergency demands that we act instantly and correctly, we simply have to depend on feel, not vision, in order to act quickly enough. The time spent looking at what we are doing is time during which our boat is travelling — very possibly at high speed — toward calamity. The essential thing to remember is to bring the blade horizontal, and to use the resultant slender profile of the oar to slow the boat.

Well executed, this method will stop the boat very quickly; as it comes to a stop, the rower is in good position to take an immediate backing stroke — often a necessity. In one continuous movement you can stop the boat and reverse direction. Every other method requires an additional movement to get the blades under water for the backing stroke without which the boat simply continues to move forward.

TURNING

The easiest way to turn a boat is to lay one blade on the water with the loom at right angles to the boat, shift a bit of weight onto it, and bring your forearm down to the corresponding knee. This will keep your boat stable while you pull with the other scull. Your boat will turn around the blade that is resting on the water.

If the turn requires a tighter radius, take the stroke as described above, and then shift your weight to the opposite side, and take a backing stroke with the scull that was at rest. Pull with one hand, then back with the other alternately, sliding the non-working blade on the surface of the water. In this way your boat will remain stable.

LANDING

Landing any boat requires good judgement and a good eye for speed and the angle of approach. Too much speed and too great an angle create hazards for the boat and the equipment. Too little speed and too shallow an angle leave the boat inconveniently distant from the dock. To get it right practise on clear open water with a floating object to represent the dock. This will eliminate the temptation to reach out of the boat in a lunge for the dock, and will teach the use of the waterside oar as a brake.

Remember that if you use the back of the blade to arrest the boat you will lift that rigger, throwing the other oar onto the dock. Turn the waterside blade *slightly* off the feather to get the leading edge underwater, and use it to push the rigger down. Working your blade in the water accomplishes two things at the same time: by slowing the boat down from one side you can turn it as it approaches the dock; by pressing the waterside handle down at the same time you lift the opposite rigger with its oar to clear the dock. It may be helpful to visualize the end of your oar as the compass point and the boat as the pencil with which you will draw an arc.

Put the blade into the water and swing the boat around parallel to the dock.

Although it is instinctive to reach out with your hand to fend off the dock as you approach it, this is the worst way to manage a safe landing. The boat will inevitably fall toward the dock. Control of the boat depends upon having the waterside blade in the water. Wait until the dockside rigger is over the dock and the boat's way is stopped or safely slowed *before* you reach out for the dock.

STEERING

Steering is course-keeping, that is, setting a mark to steer by, estimating the longest safe, straight-line distance you can row, and rowing that distance along that line. Look over the bow to establish the course, then look astern for a mark to steer by and then row away. The fact that the boat veers to one side of the course or the other has nothing to do with any inadequacy of the boat nor any imbalance in the physique of the rower. It wanders because pressure is not being applied equally with each blade. That will correct itself with time, so long as you develop the habit of watching for any side-to-side movement of the stern. Underway, it is best to turn to look where you are going during the recovery, not during the stroke.

SPECIAL SKILLS

STANDING PUSHOFF

The best way to move your boat away from the dock is to shove off with your leg while standing up. You simply remain standing after you have taken the scull handles in your waterside hand, ends butted together. Put the other hand on the gunwale, transfer your weight to the boat, crouch slightly on the leg you are standing on and, placing your other foot on the edge of the dock, give a vigorous push. Make sure that the water-side blade is resting on the surface, tip up, so that you can ride it until your dockside blade clears. You will then have both blades on the water. Sit down quickly, without attempting to put your dockside foot in the clog or shoe. Instead, extend that foot over the stretcher and use the weight of your leg for balance. In this way you will be able to let your weight down gracefully, pulling from the handles and from the gunwales.

SCULLING THE BOAT SIDEWAYS

Suppose there is only a limited space in which to land your boat. Approaching at an appropriate angle to land in that space will be impossible because the dockside blade has to be kept clear of other boats and rowers. Is there another way? Yes, if you are willing to accept a little risk and spend time practising one-blade sculling. Find some quiet water, not too far from land. It is easy to roll over in a racing single while you are learning to do this, so it is wise to make your first attempts in a wherry.

Start out by passing one handle back and forth with the blade resting on the water, turning up the leading edge of the blade at every change of direction. Get the feel of the balance of the boat and prepare to use the weight of the other oar in the rowlock for balance when you move to step two. Next, while passing the first blade to and fro, reverse its pitch so that the leading edge enters the water *at a very slight angle*. You will immediately feel pressure on the face of the blade. This will cause the handle to rise. Apply downward pressure on the handle while leaning away to maintain your balance. Lift the opposite blade off the water because you will want it to pass over the dock. Look away from the blade you are working. This will pass the control of the blade from your eyes to your hands.

Keep the handle moving, reversing the pitch of the blade each time to keep constant pressure on the face of it through-out the movement. Gradually, increase the pressure on the blade by moving the handle with more force. Very soon you will discover that your boat is moving sideways. Now, if you can keep the opposite blade off the water consistently, you will have achieved the balance you will need in order to approach a landing sideways. If you have inclined your blade at too great an angle, your boat will move forward and backward—not sideways. Everything depends on controlling the pressure on the face of the blade. That pressure has to be exactly equalled by the weight of your body leaning away from it. It helps to keep your eyes fixed on a target point or the dock and so depend on the feel of the water on the blade.

SCULLING IN ROUGH WATER

Sculling in rough water requires that you be light and quick with your hands. If you have any tendency to grip your handles, rough water and the fear of capsizing will only aggravate it. Only a light hold will allow your hands to respond instantly and surely to every encounter of the blade with a random wave. Offer as little resistance as possible to avoid the quick rise of the rigger that follows the impact of the blade against a wave. You will have to clear your blades a little higher, of course. Strike your hands away while your sculls are still bent, but strike them toward your knees. The slight change of angle in the return of the handles will allow the blades to rise a little quicker and clear the next wave. Pulling a blade through the water creates a pocket of turbulence behind it, levelling the water and tearing down any waves, making it easy to clear your blade.

Rowing in rough water is a good test of skill. What you could get away with on calm water—deficiencies of technique that hardly seem to matter—will become glaringly obvious. You are confronted with a choice: to avoid rough water at any cost, or to look at rough water as an opportunity to test and refine your sculling skills. For a small, light sculler rough water does not present as great a hazard as it does for a large, heavy sculler whose weight sinks the boat and reduces freeboard. Still, if you are feeling apprehensive, choose a wherry.

TROUBLE AFLOAT

A waterman learns quickly the ways of wind and water. He has to know the winds that prevail where he chooses to row, when they arise, from what quarter they pose the greatest threat, how they shift, how they are shaped by local terrain. A sculler setting out must know how he is going to make it back. There will be no coach nor rescue craft standing by to look after him if he is prevented from returning home by contrary wind or dangerous waves, nor if he rolls over.

As a sculler you have a responsibility to stay out of trouble. You are in the most vulnerable boat afloat, so it is you who have the most to lose in any situation involving another boat. Let me suggest a few ways I have found to avoid or minimize damage to my boat or myself.

MOTOR BOAT APPROACHING FROM AHEAD

Upon sighting the vessel, large or small, towing a threatening wake, move away from its projected course. As the first wave comes near turn *parallel* to it so that it the boat will lift evenly. Keep both blades in light contact with the water and let the handles move upward and downward as the wave passes under you.

MOTOR BOAT APPROACHING FROM ASTERN
Change course 30 to 40 degrees away from the projected
course of the vessel until its wake is nearly upon you, then
turn back toward the motor boat in order to meet the first
wave parallel to it. Rowing diagonally away gives you more
time to put distance between yourself and the oncoming
wake than you would have if you turned at right angles.
In the wake, stop rowing and play the handles loosely as
your boat rises and falls.

CATCHING A CRAB SCULLING
To catch a crab, or crabbing, is to catch the water with the
leading edge of the blade, driving it under. The way to avoid
a crab is to use a light, firm hold on your sculls.
    Use very little wrist to take the blades out of the
water. Strike the handles away sharply with firm wrists,
just slightly flexed. The feathering of your sculls must *follow*
the extraction of your blades, when you open your hands
and let your sculls fall onto the feather and rest on the sill
of the rowlocks. You will probably catch a crab if you grip
your handles too tightly. Although a good sculler can catch
a crab without losing his balance, many people will go over
the side. The coaming of a single, particularly a wooden
one, is very vulnerable to the impact of a falling body, so if
you lose your balance, go limp and slide out of your boat
like an otter. Deal with the next order of business, reboarding,
as philosophically as possible.

REBOARDING A SINGLE FROM THE WATER
Assuming that you have lost control of one handle and are
falling to that side, hold onto the other handle as you go into
the water. Your boat will move away from you as you fall out
of it. When you come to the surface face your boat and pull

yourself toward it, hand over hand on the scull. Right the boat if necessary. Gather up both handles in the same hand and make sure that both scull collars are set firmly against the rowlocks.

Position yourself beside the rower's bench and put your other hand in the middle of the bench aft of the seat which will have rolled aft. Keep the blades bearing on the water, then let yourself sink in the water and, with a kick, surge up, torso across the boat as close as possible to the riggers, centering your weight on the bench. Keep your weight away from the coamings. At this moment you ought to stop and re-establish the balance by making sure the blades are both in contact with the water. It usually happens that they are not. Carefully twist your body around until you face the stern and let your legs straddle the boat without allowing them to bear heavily on the coaming. Keeping as much weight as possible on the hand centered on the rower's bench, bring your legs through the water on either side of the boat and one at a time back in the boat. The seat should be nudging your hand, meanwhile, where it is in position to receive your weight.

There are variations on this maneuver but they are best practised in warm water in a boat like the Pocock trainer. A particularly athletic and well-coordinated person can vault from the water, twisting into position over the seat, and drop neatly into it, all in one motion. It is possible to enter the boat from the water over the aft end of the cockpit. With the handles secure in one hand you can place your other hand on the middle of the cross-brace joining the back stays of the riggers across the boat and pull yourself over it. Then, rolling on your back, you can wriggle under the handles. This method has the advantage that it is easier to keep the blades bearing on the water this way. It has the disadvantage that it is hard on your back as you writhe across the brace.

REBOARDING A WHERRY FROM THE WATER
Although it is rare that a person will roll out of wherry, it does happen. A man arranged a sculling lesson with me one day and brought his wife along to watch. I thought she would enjoy the time more if she too got in a boat. Fifteen minutes after they had both embarked in wherries, the husband had fallen out of his boat. His wife was managing without any difficulty. The man was handicapped by his size and a certain amount of tension which manifested itself in his strenuous grip on the sculls. His wife, smaller, and with a lower center of gravity, seemed relaxed and willing to let the boat and the oars tell her what to do.

Well, I wasn't at hand when my pupil went over, but we were on a small river and he was close to shore when he capsized. He stood on the bottom, righted the boat and got back in unassisted. In deep water, too far from land to try to reach it by swimming alongside the boat, his situation would have been very different.

Wherries with proper buoyancy tanks will float when they are swamped and support a major part of the weight of most rowers. However, getting into one from the water requires some means of stabilizing it. Once it has been righted, the rower's bench is too wide to reach across, so the effort of crawling in at midships usually rolls it over. The best way is to go to one end, preferably the bow, and by pushing it down hard a few times, force as much water out of the boat as possible. Grasp the tops of both sides, close to the bow, and pull yourself over one side while keeping the boat level, to keep water from coming in amidships. Once in the boat, you can crawl along the bottom and, keeping your weight low, reach out near the rowlocks for the handles, one at a time, and draw them into the boat, keeping them snug in the rowlocks. Only then should you try to get back on the seat. It is necessary to have the handles in one hand and the blades on the water, feathered, stabilizing the boat before you raise your weight from the bottom of the boat.

HITTING THINGS

Racing shells are very quiet. Other rowers can be on you before you hear them or see them. The first concern, should you meet head-on, is to avoid injuring each other.

Let us suppose that you have suddenly heard the splash of a bow wave or blade close ahead. Immediately stop rowing, set your blades on the feather and start them into the water. When you have arrested the way of the boat—and only then—look around. You are now in position to divert your boat to left or right as necessary, or to begin backing away.

On one occasion I encountered a double. It was approaching so fast and so close—about two feet off my port side—that I decided to roll my boat over in order to clear the oar and rigger on that side. I crabbed my starboard blade to start the boat over and swung the port handle to line up with the center line of the boat. This took care of the possibility that my oar might strike the bow oarsman in the back. The double shot past, with their port sculls trailing, just ticking my rigger but doing no damage. I, of course, was on my way into the water.

After they had passed, the double came back and brought the after part of the coaming close to me. With one hand on it and the other on my rower's bench I lifted myself back in my boat. No harm done to either boat or crew.

PUTTING IT ALL TOGETHER
IMAGERY

I think we all look for appropriate imagery to help focus our thinking. Good sculling conjures up in my mind images drawn from the arts. Bowing a violin. And the ballet: movement and gesture subordinated to music, effort transcended by grace. The ideal stroke is seamless, without beginning or end. In music, dance and, most of all, in nature, seamlessness, spontaneity, and precision guarantee survival and characterize mastery.

One of my most pleasant memories is of a squad of Lake Washington Rowing Club women I was coaching in 1968 in preparation for the national women's championships, held in Philadelphia that year.

For a long time I had tried to shape their movements so that they could make the transitions from explosive effort at the catch to complete relaxation on the recovery. They seemed never to be ready at the catch because they slumped on their slides between strokes. They had difficulty reaching out properly and they washed out their blades. They were, in a word, graceless. One day I told them straight out that they needed to learn good carriage and posture. "Watch ballet," I said.

A week later, when we met on the water to begin our workout, five smiling faces greeted me. "Guess what, Frank?"

"Can't possibly."

"We've all been to the ballet!"

"Show me."

They started off, transformed. Heads were up, backs lengthened, stretched out from the hips to make the catch. Their rowing was lively; they were enjoying themselves. At the national championships they won almost everything they entered. Perhaps the equation graceful therefore

victorious omits something. These athletes were willing to work hard and they loved to compete. But their very intensity had been creating awkwardness. With an appropriate image of themselves as dancer-athletes, they were able to control this intensity and give it efficient expression.

Good rowing doesn't look labored or deliberate; it looks spontaneous. For this reason I ask athletes to spend time at the zoo because animal movement seems to me to epitomize grace and spontaneity.

UNITY OF BOAT AND CREW

The boat should not be regarded as just a platform—and a very unstable platform at that—on which a crew sets out to do some very hard work. That attitude will produce only vexation and very poor rowing. It is much more useful to think of the boat and its crew as one entity, one system.

One of the benefits I have derived from years of watching Westerns and movie cowboys the likes of William S. Hart, Tom Mix, Buck Jones and John Wayne is that I think I know pretty well how a horse should be ridden. I was puzzling the other day why it should be that so many movie cowboys rode well. Then it came to me: the distraction created by one bad horseman as the posse gallops off in hot pursuit would ruin the whole effect. The audience would spot instantly the man who *couldn't* ride, and the drama of the chase would be lost while the audience waited for the greenhorn to fall off. No, the good rider is so much at one with his mount that he seems to have become a part of it. In spite of the fact that the animal's backbone is bending and flexing like a whip, snapping the horseman backward and forward, he reacts spontaneously to stay aboard, and to keep his weight from being unnecessarily burdensome to the horse. Good scullers treat their boats in the same way. Happily, what is good for the boat is good for the crew.

CONTROLLING YOUR BREATHING
Unlike the beating of the heart, the action of the lungs is susceptible of considerable conscious control. We might be tempted to say that breathing simply responds to the body's need for oxygen. However, breathing does have to be tended to. It's not infrequently heard that a rower forgot to breathe during the first four or five strokes of a start. Excitement and tension can bring this about. Smart coxswains tell their crews to breathe on the third or fourth stroke. In a single scull you have to be both coxswain and crew. The best way to tie your breathing cycle to the stroke cycle is to approach the catch exhaling, timing the intake of breath with the entry of the blade. This allows you to relax before each catch. Low rates provide plenty of time for relaxing; obviously, as the rate goes up there is less time, but time nevertheless. When it is necessary to take two breaths per stroke take the second breath as you swing out of the bow and exhale before the next catch. By breathing in when your chest naturally opens just

before the catch, you build into the stroke the relaxation and stillness that makes continued heavy exertion possible.

RELAXING

Stroking a double with a student at bow I was offering suggestions about gestures, specific effects we wanted to produce with the blade. "Relax." I crooned the word. I tried to mesmerize my student into a sleep-like state that would allow her to move virtually unconsciously and therefore efficiently. We produced three or four strokes that didn't roll the boat or pull it to one side or the other. It seemed a good moment to stop and consider how we achieved this. Did she notice the good strokes? "Yes." Was she aware of why they were better than the others? "Not exactly." Was she, then, more relaxed? "Yes," she said, "I relaxed my jaw."

To discover what position your arms and hands ought to take while rowing, sit at the full reach and the release position and relax. At the catch position, blades feathered and on the water, the hands should rest lightly on the handles under the second joint of the middle finger, index finger almost off the end, wrist easily straight, not bent in either plane, elbows straight but not locked, arm muscles soft.

At the finish sit with blades feathered and lying on the water, your hands resting on the handles, and check the amount of tension in the arms and hands. Relax your muscles to allow your elbows to drop. Flaring your elbows flattens your wrists and depresses the handles. Your wrists should be flexed slightly upward. Your blades should be fully covered at this point in the stroke. If it seems difficult to achieve this positioning, your shoulders may not be drawn back sufficiently. Drawing them back and down should put you in the proper position.

Rule of thumb: if at any moment during the cycle of the stroke you could stop moving and relax, the positioning of your hands and arms should remain unchanged. No muscles would be in tension that are not actively engaged in moving the oar.

A position of perfect repose in rowing comes during the recovery when the torso has moved back through the perpendicular and achieved the angle at which it will begin the stroke. At this moment virtually all your muscles find relief. As much as possible, take the curvature out of your lower back. At this moment you should feel alert readiness. For a moment there is nothing to do but let the boat run. At racing pace this moment may last but a fraction of a second, but that does not make it any less welcome or important. If your body is held perfectly still at the catch angle, your back will be prepared for the thrust of your legs. Perfect coupling of back and legs at the catch will minimize the checking of the boat.

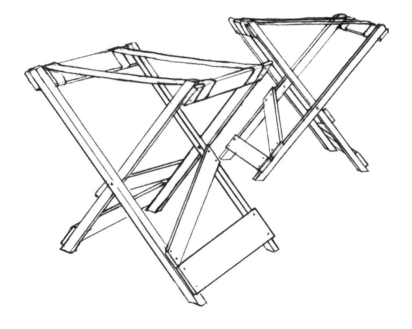

◆ BEYOND FUNDAMENTALS ◆
REFINING YOUR ROWING SKILLS
ROWING WITH EYES CLOSED

Every coach knows the value of asking a crew to row with their eyes closed. (I have an authenticated report of a coxswain who closed his eyes along with the crew!) I discovered that it is a helpful way to master such things as stopping a boat. Most people set about controlling their sculls by looking at them. However, since only one blade can be under observation at a time, the beginner may make frantic efforts to see both, losing control of first one scull, then the other in the process. In a safe stretch of water, you can practise stopping or turning the boat with your eyes closed and experience the development of control that comes with feeling what the blade is doing and what the loom is doing in the rowlock. Suddenly, it is obvious that your hands respond to subtle movements instantly, and with a bit of practise, reliably.

LISTENING TO YOUR BOAT
The single is the prima donna among boats; you must cater to its every quirk and whim. An eight is much more stable, so the rower in an eight tends to depend on other observers for clues to his own performance. The crew of an eight also responds to the boat, of course, but the effect of the individual oarsman's movements can be somewhat blurred by those of the other rowers. All this changes in a single. It has to be played like a musical instrument. Its response to its crew is instantaneous and undeniable. (For this reason it is best not to try to learn to scull in one.) The sculler who listens to his boat will learn a great deal from it.

The sound of the water breaking under the bow increases with speed. The slight turbulence of the water closing around the stern also tells you how fast the boat is going. Your ears will tell you that the boat should be rowed in such a way as to keep the sounds coming from bow and stern at a constant pitch. Impossible, of course, because of the periodic nature of the propulsion. But the effort to control your speed by listening to it will do wonders for your sculling.

The sound of your sculls shifting and turning in the rowlocks tells you whether you are keeping pressure against the rowlocks. A quiet rowlock tells you that you have a solid grip of the water as you finish the stroke and that you are not slamming your blades onto the feather. The absence of noise means that you are not feathering your blade at the end of the pull-through, but rather allowing it to roll onto the feather on the way bowward.

CONTROLLING THE WATERLINE
Depressing a boat in the water and lifting it up again wastes energy. Any vertical movement of body weight whatsoever will raise and lower the waterline, and generate waves that emanate laterally from the hull as the energy of the body's movement is transferred into the water. To eliminate this waste of energy, it is useful to isolate particular movements and to observe their effect upon the water beside the boat.

LAYBACK AND ITS EFFECT ON THE WATERLINE
Sit with your legs down, and your body upright. Swing your back to the layback position and return it to the perpendicular. Observe the propagation of waves from the side of the boat. You will see that the vertical movement of the body is having an effect upon the waterline, that is to say, the amount of hull in the water. To find how to decrease the size of the waves this movement produces, take your feet out of the clogs or shoes and lay them on top. Lean back until your feet are light on the stretcher and then quickly lean forward holding your back firm.

With nothing to hold your feet down, they will fly up in the air. To keep your feet in place send your head toward your feet, curling your back. This will minimize the upward movement of your torso. You will now observe smaller waves emanating from the sides of the boat. With this wave generation in mind, row with your feet out of the clogs or shoes until you can keep your feet bearing on the stretcher. You are now ready to learn how to use your shoulders to help you to change direction at the end of the stroke.

To discover how much motion you have available in your shoulders, sit with your legs down and straighten your arms. Using only your shoulders, move the handles forward and backward, sliding your blades on the surface of the water. Some people can move their shoulders thus only an inch or so; others can move them nearly six inches.

This shoulder mobility is extremely useful in prolonging the stroke and in aiding the transfer of weight at the end of the stroke. With it you can continue to draw your handles in and keep your weight suspended on them, even as you begin to move your body out of the bow. At the instant you feel your weight start to leave the bow, use your shoulders to propel your hands away, just as if you were throwing a two-handed punch.

WAVE - MAKING AT THE CATCH
Sit upright at the sternward end of the slide. Then, drop your body forward from the hips. Raise and lower your body in this way and observe the waves radiating from the boat. Notice as well the rise and fall of the stern. Obviously, the way to minimize wave propagation at the beginning of the stroke is to eliminate all upward and downward movement of the body.

Much of the skill you need to move a boat well is related to controlling the effect of your weight. The less you allow the boat to depart from its designed waterline, the better it will perform. At lower strokes the increase in the speed of the boat may be very small, but at racing strokes, tiny lapses from good form have a distressing and cumulative effect that rob the boat of inches of run each stroke.

TESTING FOR BACKWARD MOVEMENT
One last test will reveal the amount of check at the beginning of the stroke. Check, so called, is the backward movement of the boat in response to your forward movement in the boat at the catch. Because you are four or five times as heavy as your boat, you remain still with respect to the water, while your boat slips backward.

Position your boat perpendicular to the dock with the stern a few inches from it. Take the catch position. Make the beginning of the stroke in three ways: first, with the blades squared and buried, second, with the blades squared and off the water, and finally, with the blades flat on the water. Keeping your balance makes the second position the most difficult if you are in a single, but is in fact what most people try to do. Cut off each stroke before the handles have travelled six inches, relax, and return the boat to the original position. The object is to see how far the stern moves backward before it moves forward.

THE IDEAL CATCH
Starting the stroke with the blades already covered is the ideal way to begin; however, it can only be used for the first stroke. Many crews start races this way. Still, it gives us the minimum check, and a basis for gauging the effectiveness of the next two catches.

THE "LOGICAL" CATCH
Catching with the blades already squared above the water would seem to be the most logical way to begin, except that in practise the blades must be kept safely off the water until they change direction, so the center of 6–1/2 inch wide sculling blades will be at least 3–1/4 inches off the water. The tops of the blades will have to travel at least 6–1/2 inches downward before they are covered, during which the sculls swing through a considerable portion of their arc. Meanwhile, the thrust of your legs will drive the boat backward.

To test this effect, rest the blades in the water squared, then pop them out and catch. After a few trials, you will be able to reproduce the squared up catch as it would be in a moving boat. You will find that you have pushed the stern farther back than you did when you began the stroke with your blades covered.

THE SCULLER'S CATCH
In the third test lay the blades feathered on the water. The object is to catch as if the blades were already covered, so let your fingers turn the blade as you pull. Pulling the blades in will load them virtually as quickly as if they had already been buried and will produce a markedly shorter backward movement of the stern than did the previous experiment. The reason is that the water will turn the blades for you if your fingers are quick and light on the handle. If, as a Zen aphorism puts it, "You think that what you do not do yourself does not happen,"[4] you will fail to make use

of a valuable ally, the water itself. A reminder: any movement of the wrist slows the entry of the blade, allowing
the boat to move backward.

The gestures involved in moving a boat are extremely
subtle. To make them with the most economy of movement
and effort, depend on what you can feel and hear. The
transitions at each end of the slide have to be so smooth as to
deceive the eye, and accompanied by a spontaneous, quick
movement of the blade.

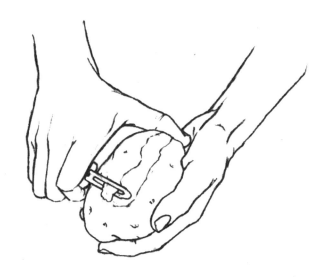

TECHNICAL TROUBLESHOOTING
TRACKING STRAIGHT

S teering can become a nearly unconscious effort if the sculler continues to train—educate—his body to work synchronously. After sculling a few hundred miles keeping the stern fixed on an aiming point, you will be prepared for the next step, keeping course with your eyes closed. The important thing in this drill is that it both prepares one for racing and reinforces and strengthens your sensed control of the sculls. Rowing straight requires even pressure, pressure that is sensed by the body. Row, say, five strokes, keeping the stern fixed on a mark, close your eyes and continue to row another five strokes. Open your eyes while continuing to row and observe the course deviation, make the appropriate correction and repeat the exercise. Over a period of a month or so, repeating this exercise on every outing, you will acquire a sharper perception of the working of each scull, hence a degree of refinement that can't be achieved in any other way.

CONTROLLING THE RIGGER HEIGHT

I often hear complaints from scullers who are having trouble clearing the port blade. The port blade will stick if the left wrist is kept flat, causing the left hand to pull through too high. This lifts the starboard rigger and depresses the port rigger, which in turn forces the right hand down. It will also be difficult to release the port blade if the left hand is pulled through ahead of the right. However, if the handle of the starboard scull is tucked behind the port by allowing the left wrist to flex upward, both handles will come back in nearly the same plane; the boat will stay level, and the port blade will no longer cause difficulty.

BLADE TRAPPED IN THE WATER

A blade becomes trapped and difficult to extract from the water when the water following the blade has caught up to it. It is as simple as that. However, as long as the oar is bent driving the water back, the blade can be freed from the water almost effortlessly. If you neglect to keep pulling to the end of the stroke, the water behind the blade catches up to it and pushes the handle toward you. You will have to fight the oar free. It seems paradoxical (like a good many things in rowing) that the safest way to deal with an oar or scull handle that is nearing the body at the limit of the draw, is not to stop pulling prior to sending it away, but to pull harder! You should concentrate on *reversing the direction of the blade* rather than lifting it out of the water. The reason is this: by changing direction instantly—not by making a downward, circular motion with your handles—but by striking the slightly-turned handles away from your body, your blades will leave the water on a slightly diagonal path through aerated water that offers no resistance.

When your blades are on their way, feather them by rolling the handles out of your hands as you learned to do with the dowel. Using your wrists to feather your blades is virtually certain to cause your blades to be trapped, because as you tip your wrists, you raise your handles.

BLADE GOING TOO DEEP AT THE BEGINNING

When your blade enters the water underpitched, it "knifes" downward: pressure on the angled face simply drives the blade down. When you grip the handle tightly you prevent the loom from seating itself in the rowlock and taking the correct angle. Loosen your hold and push the handle around with your fingers as the blade enters the water. You should feel the handle slide in your fingers in the split second that it takes to cover the blade.

I prefer to rotate the handle by lifting the second and third fingers a quarter inch or so and tapping the handle with the tips of these fingers. The handle slides in the circle of thumb and forefinger as the blade enters the water, squaring as it does so. Plainly, this method, the best one I know, depends on an absolutely relaxed hold.

BLADES GOING TOO DEEP IN THE MID-STROKE

If you experience difficulty getting your blades out cleanly, watch for water covering the looms a distance of a foot or more up from the blades at mid-stroke. Driving the blades deep forces you to pull your handles down as you finish, leaving insufficient space over your legs to allow you to get the handles away. Not that a well-covered blade isn't a good thing; it won't slip or break the surface of the water. But too much of a good thing shapes your pull-through in an arc that rises through the middle of the stroke and drops at the end of it. Some scullers can manage deep blades very well, the great Australian, Stuart McKenzie, for example, because he keeps full pressure on his blades through the release.

To correct this fault, pull downward as you begin the stroke, as if you were going to draw your handles in an inverted arc. Aim your handles at your knees. (This will encourage you to drive your legs down harder.) You will find that your handles will rise as you complete the stroke, especially if you are keeping your elbows down and letting your wrists rise.

LOOSE OR WASHED-OUT FINISH

When I see a sculler having difficulty at the finish clearing his blades smartly and efficiently, I watch the collars of his sculls to see whether he is holding them snugly against the rowlocks at the end of the stroke. Scullers, novice scullers especially, sometimes forget to push their handles away from the centerline of the boat as they finish. By drawing their hands straight back they unseat their sculls and so loosen their hold on the water. In a double with a pupil it is often the first thing I see or hear. The remedy is simple: press the sculls into the rowlocks. The blade will seem to clear itself without any help from the hand.

Another reason for a soft finish is the failure to keep your seat locked in the bow while you pivot your body out of the bow. This flaw enters the stroke when you allow your lower back to slump. It is usually accompanied by a slight rise of the knees. Your seat starts out of the bow, returns, and then moves toward the stern. To firm up your finish, press your legs hard against the rower's bench until you have pivoted your torso from your hips and started it out of the bow.

STERN CHECK
Your shell checks backward at the beginning of every stroke because of the thrust of your legs against the stretcher. Use the turbulence at the stern of your boat to gauge the amount of this inevitable hesitation. To minimize it be quick to get your blades covered; avoid swinging your back down before the catch, or swinging it up too quickly as you make the catch. Row to keep the stern from rising or falling.

INJURY TROUBLESHOOTING
CAUSES OF INJURIES

Injuries are as common among experienced athletes as beginners and can often be traced to errors in technique. Many injuries are superficial but irritating, and can easily be avoided. Serious injuries often follow from injudicious weight training and from the failure to warm up for heavy exertion. Rowing with such injuries only delays healing.

FOREARM TIGHTNESS AND TENDINITIS
Apprehension causes tension. The sculler whose wrists and forearms are sore is gripping the handles because he is apprehensive about losing control of his sculls and the boat. Lay your open hand on one scull, and, keeping your hand and forearm in a straight line, move the blade back and forth above the water. After a few passes, drop the blade to the surface and curl the fingers quickly around the handle with the idea of kicking the handle around rather than twisting it around to make the catch. Begin using the legs to start the stroke, letting the fingers react spontaneously as they are keyed by the leg-drive to take the water. Catch only when your wrist lies in the line from the second joint of the second finger to the elbow, and only when your hand and arm are completely relaxed. To return the blade, simply push the handle away, allowing your wrist to tip *only a few degrees*. Straighten your wrist immediately, lifting the "basket" of your fingers, and let the blade roll onto the feather. At the first sign of gripping, dropping the wrist, or tension, discontinue the drill. Relax and try again.

I have heard the suggestion that tight forearms are caused by lack of muscular strength, and that the remedy is to work with weights. Nothing could be farther from the truth. The remedy for pain in any muscle is relaxation. To avoid pain learn how to use the muscles efficiently. Good technique allows the muscles of the forearms to rest throughout most of the stroke cycle. If the handle is not gripped, a minimum of muscular activity is involved in managing the scull or oar, even on the pull-through. Gripping the handle ensures that the forearm muscles are always in tension. With tension comes fatigue, pain, and loss of control.

INJURIES TO BACK AND RIBS
Injuries to backs and ribs may have their origin in bad posture, or in strenuous off-water weight training, improperly prescribed or carried out. For these injuries the athlete has no recourse but medical treatment. Rowing properly, however, prevents injuries. If the therapists who treat injured athletes could spend an hour or two in the coaches' launches they would see clearly why rowers are coming to them. There is overwhelming evidence that many coaches are arbitrary about the ways they want their athletes to move. In shaping them to their personal ideal, such coaches ride roughshod over their obligation to protect their athletes from injury.

Make the beginning of the stroke with your lower back pressed down and your belly squashing into your thighs. Remember the image of the orange being squeezed.

Lengthening your back as I have explained will prevent injury and excessive fatigue. If the muscles of your back are allowed to lengthen and contract rhythmically during the stroke cycle, they will perform better. Changing their length protects them; keeping them fixed and rigid invites spasm.

Similarly, the proper use of your back will protect your ribs and the muscles over them from injury. If you make the beginning of your pull-through with a slight lifting of your sternum, you will firm your upper spine and direct the pull to the muscles across your back that are best able to take the load. Injury to your rib cage is then virtually impossible. Catching with your chest folded over your knees risks injury and impairs your breathing. Let your chest have the room it needs by letting it pass between your knees. (Of course, you don't want your knees to fall outward, either. Let them meet your armpits and your legs will be well aligned for the drive.)

When rowing a sweep, use your back as symmetrically as possible. Even though you have to follow the oar out of the boat with the hand that is at the end of the handle, don't twist your spine to increase your reach. Don't lean toward your rigger. Both these movements compound the curve in your back, creating vastly dissimilar strains on either side of it. So, although sweep rowing is an asymmetrical activity, use your body as it functions best, symmetrically.

DRILLS

D rills generally have as their object a particular element in the management of the body weight, the oar or the boat. Because they draw attention to a part of the stroke, rather than to the unity of the whole, they have to be used judiciously. The perfect stroke is a perfect gesture: seamless, spontaneous, graceful.

FIXED SLIDE
Rowing with a fixed slide, legs down, swing through as much of the stroke as you can manage, emphasizing the quick return of your body to the catch position after each stroke. Pause before going into the water, with your arms extended, to preserve a ratio that allows twice as much time for the recovery as for the pull-through. Although there should be a sharp angle at the hips, it won't do to try to extend the reach by bending the back. Once your back is elongated and still, make no further effort to move it.

This drill can be used to quicken the movement of the weight of the torso out of the bow. Holding a good position a moment before the blade goes in acts to eliminate dropping the body, lunging at the catch.

When I first considered this drill, it seemed that the strongest reason for using it was to practise getting the body started back through the upright position while the weight was on the handles. I have since discovered that scullers often interpret the drill to mean that the handles are to be returned as rapidly as possible, to the point that they cut the stroke short in order to do it. I have since gone about presenting this drill in a very different way. At arms' length from the handles hurl yourself into the bow, attempting to get as much propulsion from the weight of your torso as possible. Pretend you are in a dory loaded with fish or nets or whatever, trying to get to shore ahead of an approaching storm. Pull with all your might, pull as though your life depended on

THE CATCH (RIGHT)

THE CATCH (WRONG)

it. Once you have succeeded in driving the boat just as hard as you can, consider what effect your exertions are having on the waterline. You will in fact be "sousing" the bow. Now, maintain the same effort as before, and at the same time control the waterline by pressing your handles home with your shoulders. The souse will disappear and you will discover that you are not chinning yourself to the handles with your arms, but instead squeezing your shoulder blades to reverse the movement of your back. Someone outside the boat can easily observe the effect on the waterline. You, yourself, will know that the waterline is being controlled if your feet remain in solid contact with the stretcher.

FEET OUT OF THE CLOGS
The purpose of this drill is to emphasize the importance of getting your weight out of the bow while your sculls are bent. Take your feet out of the shoes or clogs and lay them on top. Row to keep your feet from lifting.

If you have set your back stops properly, your seat wheels will just touch them as you finish the stroke. If your back stops are too far behind you, you will drift helplessly away from your stretcher as soon as your blades leave the water. Not a comfortable feeling. Eliminate this drift by shifting the tracks so that the back stops are close to the wheels. If you can feel the wheels pressing against the stops when you pivot out of the bow, the movement of your body sternward will shove the boat forward. If you send your arms away quickly and curl your back, you will find that you can keep your feet from rising.

HALF - SLIDE
The purpose of the half-slide drill is to accustom yourself to preparing for the catch by being absolutely still. To find half slide, locate the midpoint between the limits of the actual length of the track you use, *not* the midpoint of the entire

MID-STROKE (RIGHT)

MID-STROKE (WRONG)

track. Position yourself, then, at half slide and establish the angle of your body exactly as it is when you catch at full slide, using only half the slide. Begin to scull at a low rate, say twenty strokes per minute, taking as much time between strokes as you would at full slide. This does not mean to use the whole period of the recovery to complete your swing to the catch position. In fact, use as little time as possible. You will discover that, if you start squeezing your belly between your legs as soon as you swing through the upright position, your back will be properly aligned, just as you arrive at half slide. Pause there with your arms extended and your body quite still until it is time to catch.

Resist the impulse to add more body angle as you make the catch. If you have been in the habit of completing your body swing only at the last moment before you catch, you will find this difficult. A variation of this drill will improve your balance. Rowing full slide, begin and end each stroke at half slide, pausing for one or two or three counts before proceeding to the catch. The quicker you get to half slide, the easier it is to balance the boat. Keep practising until you can complete the stroke without touching your blades to the water on the recovery.

ARMS AND SHOULDERS

Sit at the finish of the stroke, legs down, your back at the end of its swing, arms extended. Position your right hand under your left wrist. Row without moving any part of your body but your arms and shoulders. Be quick to catch and keep your blades covered as long as you possibly can. Pause with your arms extended before each catch. Maintain as much pressure on the blade as you can, as you complete the stroke. You will find that by drawing your shoulders forcefully back you can move the boat farther than you can with your arms alone. Use your shoulders to "punch" your hands away and your blades will slip out of the water crisply.

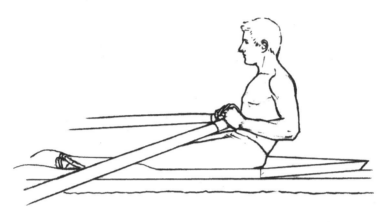

NEAR-FINISH (RIGHT)

NEAR-FINISH (WRONG)

CATCH AS CATCH CAN
This drill is intended to force you to get into position to start the stroke as quickly as possible. It requires the participation of another person, not necessarily a coach, to tell you when to catch as you row along, giving the command at arbitrary moments in the recovery, trying, as a matter of fact, to take you unaware.

As you will very soon learn, it is not possible to begin the stroke until your hands are well past your knees and separated at least five or six inches. It behooves you, then, to get to that position as soon as you can, and reinforces the importance of getting your weight quickly out of the bow.

This drill goes a long way toward producing the springiness and liveliness of good sculling, in contrast to the delay in the bow and the deliberateness that characterizes bad sculling.

CATCH ONLY
This drill is designed to develop full thrust instantaneously. Start out by positioning yourself a little short of full slide, but with the boat slightly canted, supported by light pressure on one blade. With the other scull, starting in the feathered position, try to develop a quick bend in the loom, cutting the stroke off after about four inches. When you can do this without using your wrist or moving the rigger up or down, switch to the other scull. Go on to using both sculls, stopping the boat after each trial. Apply more and more pressure until you have lifted yourself off the seat.

The object, of course, is to develop the quickest possible catch. Leap away from the stretcher *before, not after* you turn the blade up. To put it another way, catch as if the blade were already in the water.

HALF - BLADE SCULLING

In this drill you will use only the lower half of your blades. The purposes of this drill are to minimize the upward and downward movement of the handles, to ensure a level pull-through, and to develop quickness at the catch.

Start at the catch, blades feathered. Drive yourself as quickly as you can away from the stretcher. Close your fingers to rotate the sculls in response to the shove with your legs. *Do not square up your blades before you shove.* Only by using your fingers reflexively can you produce enough speed on the blade to cause it to break and tumble the water the instant it starts sternward.

Continue through the stroke, maintaining the same turbulence on the submerged half of the blade until the end of the stroke. The throats of your sculls, where the looms meet the blades, should appear to ride the surface of the water.

Doing this drill from a full stop, one stroke at a time, is easiest. The resistance offered by the water makes it easy to tear it, but only if the blade is started at rest on the feather. A lightning-quick hook, with the fingers acting in reflex to the shove with the legs works much better than trying to place the blade with the wrists. A good example of letting small muscles manage small, precise movements, rather than trying to get the same precision from large muscles. Move on to rowing continuously at half blade. When you have succeeded in producing an even tumble of water ahead of your blades, proceed to cover them. When they become quiet they will be at the correct depth.

Although it will feel as though you are pulling through lower at mid-stroke and much higher at the finish, you will be pulling through level, and your catch will have become quicker and more solid.

THE RACING START
This start is different from what may be called a regular start because it is used to get your boat up to speed as quickly as possible. A racing start usually takes the form of a series of strokes of different lengths, usually determined by the fractional amount of slide to be used to make each one.

For example, the first two strokes may be taken from half slide, the third from two-thirds. By the sixth stroke, you are at full slide.

I prefer a start that makes use of a slightly shortened first stroke, say from three-quarter slide, to overcome the inertia of the boat. Take the second stroke as soon as your hands are separated six to eight inches on the way out to the catch. Let the interval between the end of the first pull-through and the end of the second pull-through determine the cadence of successive strokes. As you progress through the ensuing strokes, try to get farther and farther down the slide in the same amount of time. The amount of slide you use, then, is determined by the speed of the boat.

It is easier to move in an established rhythm. On your way to the starting line, you need only row the first two strokes in order to polish your racing start. The rest will fall into place as soon as you start the race. In doubles and quads practising the first two strokes will quickly establish the starting cadence and gets the crew together.

COUNTERMOTION
In rowing there are several moments when one part of your body moves in one direction while another part moves in the opposite direction. This countermotion is very useful when you put it to the right use, but a bit of a nuisance when it turns up where you don't need it, like trying to put on your trousers while you are standing on one pant leg. There are two moments in the stroke when motion in two directions at the same time is especially valuable.

The first appears just as the handles approach the body. The stroke is completed and the body returned without any consequent interruption in the speed of the boat. To accomplish this, draw your handles home with the shoulders, squeezing your shoulder blades together while your back is being arrested at the end of the swing. Your back then travels through the shoulders on the way out of the bow. The easiest way to master this move is to row with the feet out of the shoes or clogs. In order to keep your feet in contact with the stretcher, to get the weight back onto them as quickly as possible, you must keep the whole weight of your body on the handles as long as possible. Without countermotion—the shoulders moving forward, the back moving aft—your weight comes off the handle and has to be picked up by the stomach muscles, lifting your feet from the stretcher, depressing the bow. Practise will produce in time a nice, continuous flowing motion out of the bow.

The other moment in the stroke when you should make use of countermotion occurs as you pass through half slide during the recovery. As you stretch out over your toes press your seat toward the bow by rotating your hips. This will elongate and "stack up" your back. It is important to continue to keep rotating your hips all the way down the slide to the catch. If you do not, your back will bend at the first thrust of the legs. At this moment it is very vulnerable to injury. Pushing the seat behind you will slow the arrival of your seat at the after-end of the slide and minimize check, the interruption of the boat's forward motion.

Properly used, countermotion produces fluid, seamless, spontaneous movement as in the two instances above. However, at two places in the stroke inappropriate countermotion interferes with good blade work. If you bring your handles out to the catch with your wrists depressed behind them, your handles will go downward as you turn them, and your wrists will move upward. Further, you will have to lift your arms to bring your blades back to the water. Two motions counter to each other, and the blades still have to be dropped into the water.

Because the essence of a good catch is quickness, it is better to hinge the rotation of your handles at the base of your fingers than at your wrists. Your handles will remain in the same plane while they are being rotated. Furthermore, your handles will already be advanced and the blades started into the water as you begin to pull. No extraneous motion; no missed water.

At the other end of the stroke, using your wrists to feather your blades does not take your handles down. Quite the opposite: it actually lifts the handles. You must then drop your handles by dropping your arms.

It is quite common to see blades rowed out so they can be feathered when they are free of the water, an inefficient way out of the difficulty. The better—and much easier—way is to firm your wrists after the blades are turned a little at the end of the stroke, and send the handle away with a firm shove from the base of your fingers, straightening your wrists at the same time. Your blades will turn themselves onto the feather if they are held lightly. Notice that your blades are to be rotated slightly *before* they are extracted. Only in this way will they slip out of the water without washing out or backing water.

FROM SCULLS TO SWEEPS

F our scullers can learn to row a four much more easily and and quickly than four oarsmen can learn to scull a quad. It is easy to see why. The sculler has two trained hands to apply to rowing on either port or starboard, where the rower has only one hand that is skilled at turning the oar. Indeed many oarsmen never change sides.

Your first experience of a larger boat may in all probability come in a pair, four, or eight simply because doubles are rare and quads rarer. You may have a few moments of awkwardness, but good sculling technique adapts very easily to good rowing. In fact, the preparation of rowers ought to begin with sculling boats.

THE HOLD AND MANAGEMENT OF THE SWEEP

Lay your oar on the water cupped upward, feathered, with the handle at arm's length. Place the middle joints of your fingers on the top of the handle, one hand flush with the end, the other a hand's breadth or so from the first. Hold your wrists straight but relaxed. They ought never to bend laterally, even when you are fully extended at the reach. Curl your fingers in a loose hook around the oar. Set your thumb lightly on the underside of the handle. The pull of both hands will be focused on the middle joints of your middle fingers, the central bearing points of your two "hooks."

To rotate the blade into position to pull, firm the wrist of the hand nearest the rowlock (the inside hand) and use your fingers to slide the handle across your thumb. Allow the handle to turn in the fingers of your outside hand. If the oar has not turned enough to bring the flat part of the oar sleeve solidly against the rowlock face (the vertical face of the rowlock), drop the oar to the feathered position and relocate your inside hand by lowering your wrist slightly, letting your fingers slip around the handle. Keep your

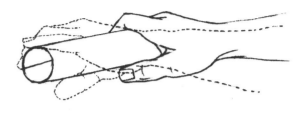

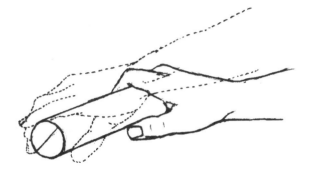

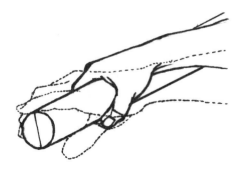

thumb in the same relative position. Do not let the web of your thumb touch the handle. If this is impossible, give some thought to finding a smaller handle.

From the new position again rotate the handle, sliding it as before across your thumb. The flat of the sleeve should now engage the face of the rowlock squarely. And if it doesn't? *If you hold the handle in your fingers, not in your fist,* the pressure of the water against the blade will settle the oar squarely for you at the instant of the catch.

THE REACH
To achieve your longest effective reach let your lockside arm fall outside the lockside knee, and extend your outside arm as far as you can through your knees. Be sure to keep the fingers of your outside hand hooked around the handle.

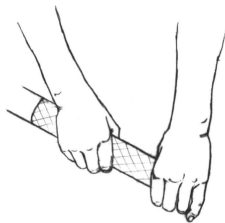

THE CATCH
You already know from your sculling what you can accomplish with quick, light hands. You have learned to use them reflexively. Begin the stroke by jumping on the stretcher before the oar comes square in the rowlock, so that you can feel it happen. Let the water do most of the work. Discover for yourself how little you have to do to square the blade. Learn to depend on the reflex action of your fingers.

THE FINISH
To complete the stroke you must draw the handle as close to your body as you can get it. Since you have committed a good deal of your body weight to the bow of the boat by shoving your legs down and leaning past the perpendicular, you have to keep pulling to keep that weight off the bow and get that weight back on the stretcher. To accomplish this you will have to use each hand differently.

As the handle approaches your body, it assumes a stronger and stronger angle. The outer end of it is substantially higher than the lockside end. In order to keep your blade covered, keep your outside elbow down. Use your shoulder to bring your handle to your body. Keep the pull of your outer hand centered under the second joint of your middle finger and let your wrist bend upward and away from your body. Do *not* allow your wrist to bend laterally! You will feel the handle sliding in your fingers and, if you look down at your hand, you will see your thumb pointing down the loom toward the blade.

This will not be the case if you have lifted your elbow, gripped your handle, or tried to keep your knuckles lined up with the axis of the oar. The first will weaken the pull, preventing your shoulder from pressing the handle home. The latter two will tend to push your body off the centerline of the boat. Obviously, it is better to keep your weight over the keel to balance the boat and to complete the stroke using your back symmetrically.

Use your inside hand just as you would with a scull. The only difference is that your thumb is under rather than across the lower edge of the end of the grip. Draw the top of the handle over as in sculling to prepare the blade to leave the water. Your wrist will flex downward just a little. Strike the handle smartly away with the roots of your fingers while holding your wrist solidly firm. As the blade leaves the water, scrub the handle across your thumb and "rap on the door" with your wrist, flattening it, and relax your fingers. The oar should fall onto the feather. If it doesn't, nudge it with your thumb.

So far, I have described the method that I have always used and coached. As I turn and send the handle away with my inside hand I let the handle carry the outside hand away. Another way to send the handle away is to use the outside hand. The inside hand turns the blade as before, but it is the outside hand that reverses the oar's direction. This alternative method distributes the effort of returning the oar, and it virtually eliminates any tendency to turn the blade too far, crabbing it. Either method will enable you to keep pressure on the blade and prevent injury.

In rowing, as in sculling, the only way to maintain control of the weight of your body and its effect on the waterline of the boat is to have a good hold. Except for a moment at each end of the stroke when the fingers of your inside hand squeeze the handle slightly to start turning the blade, your hands should be quite relaxed. If you grip your handle you cannot get the blade into the water quickly, nor keep it working long enough; your fingers lose the feel of the blade in the water or out of it, and consequently the sense of complete control that touch alone brings.

POSITIONING THE STRETCHER

In rowing, the farther your oar handle projects across your body at the finish of the stroke, the less effective you will be in maintaining pressure on your blade with your outside arm. Moving your stretcher toward the bow will bring the end of the handle and your outside hand closer to the center of your body. You will then be able to complete the stroke without twisting your body away from the handle. The important thing is to maintain the symmetrical use of your body.

EIGHTS AND FOURS

As a member of the crew of a four or an eight you are dependent on the coxswain for some clues to your performance, but not all. The coxswain can tell how much work you are doing by observing the mound of water on the face of your blade. He can tell whether you are in time by comparing the motion of your oar with the stroke's oar. He can see whether you are leaning out of the boat and whether the loom of your oar stays parallel with the other oars on your side of the boat, both of which affect the balance of the boat.

The coxswain depends on you when your boat is approaching or leaving the dock, or in any circumstance that demands a quick and precise response. Observe the effect your oar is having on the positioning of the boat whenever you are called on to use it, just as you would if you were in a single. Most of the responsibility for rowing well remains with you. You can watch your blade to see that it is at the correct depth until you can gauge its depth accurately by the feel of the oar in your hands. You can watch the stroke's oar in order to keep in time until you can feel the rhythm passing through the boat and learn to rely on the feel of it entirely. Sit over the keel. If your rigger starts to move downward it is preferable to let your blade touch the water slightly and resist the downward movement of your handle with your thumbs rather than to lean out of the boat.

If you are the stroke oar, you will be aware of the effects of bad timing. If any member of the crew catches late, you will experience an additional load as you begin the stroke without his help. If a crew member catches early, you will feel the boat move out from under your feet, depriving you of a solid platform to push against. *Make no attempt to match your timing to the crew behind you.* Your job is to set the stroke rate and rhythm, not to blend your efforts with theirs.

The eight-oared shell, like the quadruple scull, goes so fast that the pull-through passes very quickly. There is no time to dally at the end of the stroke.

CATCHING A CRAB ROWING

It is not often the case that rowers practise catching crabs—too bad—so most people are taken by surprise by their first one. It can come as a nasty shock. In a race it can effectively take a crew out of the competition. However, it, like many of life's little setbacks, can be dealt with effectively and safely. To begin with, don't resist it. Don't fight the handle. Let it pass over your shoulder. To resist is to risk being taken out of the boat. Left to itself, the oar will come to rest parallel to the boat, trailing in the water. The boat loses very little speed.

To recover the oar requires only the cooperation of the rower next behind the crabber, who must allow the crabbing rower to reach out for his handle, lie down and pass it over his body. The blade will be facing away from the boat so it is impossible to recover the oar just by pulling the handle back aboard. Assuming that the rest of the crew continues to row, the rower who has recovered his oar times his re-entry to match the crew's rhythm. At no time will his oar seriously interfere with any other. The crabbing rower must roll the handle away from him as he drops it down, lifting the blade out of the water and then rolling it 180 degrees onto the feather.

A WORD TO COXSWAINS

It is your responsibility to know each oarsman's strengths and weaknesses and their effect on his rowing. You must know exactly how to help each one to do his best work. In races, resist the temptation to give play-by-play accounts of the competition's position, stroke rate, et cetera. This is information you may have to act on but it must not be allowed to interfere with the crew's concentration. Get the boat to run true. If it ever ran true in practise with loose tiller lines, it should do so in a race. If the boat veers or rolls, find out why. Correct poor timing, missed water, dumped finishes. Be as sensitive to the needs of the boat and crew as a jockey is to his horse. The best jockey is not the one who uses the whip the

hardest. Help your crew to do their work with quiet remind-
ers to each oarsman—build their confidence. Shouting does
not oil the machinery.

PAIR ROWING
Although the most difficult of all team boats to keep upright
in and steer, the pair is still a particularly useful boat in which
to learn to row well. A crew new to this type of boat should
find some quiet backwater and become acquainted with each
other's movements and perceptions. In this uniquely inti-
mate experience they have to function like the two halves of
a single body. This requires a good deal of experimentation
and sharpening of the senses.

RIGGER CONTROL
One way to begin is to set one rower to rowing while the
other sits quietly, holding his oar lightly in order to sense the
slightest change in rigger height as the boat moves in a circle.
When the first rower can manage a stroke without deflecting
the rigger up or down, let the other rower do the same. Then

take five or ten strokes together. The results may be disappointing because a level boat running true won't be achieved so easily. The rowers will load their oars unevenly at the catch, and, at the finish release the water from unequally loaded blades. They may be returning the oar at different rates, or the weight of their oars may not strike each rigger simultaneously.

SYNCHRONIZING THE CATCHES

Back to rowing in circles. One rower should attempt a series of catches in which he tries to cover the blade as quickly as possible, drawing the handle six inches or so and releasing, always maintaining control of rigger height. Alternate as before. Each rower should by now have a good perception of the other's catch and how to attain synchrony. Row together, driving the oar in with the legs, ending the stroke as soon as the oar is bent. If you have to move the handle more than six inches to bend the oar—to fully load it—you are not moving quickly enough. Loosen your hold, relax your arms, and try again.

FINISH AND RELEASE

Both rowers sit at the finish, legs down, both blades covered, handles on the body. Bow can easily see if stroke's shoulders are down and back, elbows falling easily by the sides, and can judge how high the handle is on stroke's body. Any tension can be pointed out and corrected. Then stroke looks around to see where bow's handle is and whether his hands lie easily on the handle. Next, row using back and arms only, by turns, striving to reach the positioning agreed upon, holding as much pressure on the oar as possible, and extracting the blade cleanly.

Rowing thereafter at light pressure should proceed more satisfactorily, once each rower has had the benefit of the other's undivided attention.

STEERING WITH A RUDDER

Coxed pairs, and frequently, pairs without coxswain are fitted with rudders. But because of the resistance a rudder offers to forward progress, it should be used sparingly, more like the trim tab one sees on airplanes than as a device for making sharp turns. In a crosswind, for example, a rudder can be used to check drift.

If it becomes necessary to alter course, the rudder may be used during the pull-through when the boat is most stable. However, it is preferable for one rower to pull a little harder until the boat is on course, adding to its speed. If both rowers keep a mark in sight over the stern, they can steer as easily as a single sculler.

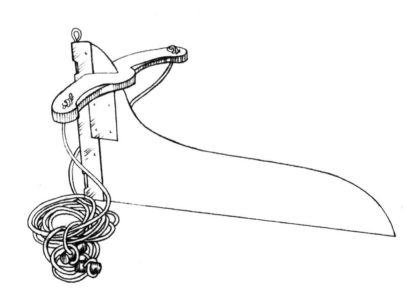

EQUIPMENT AND RIGGING

CHOOSING A BOAT

S hould you choose a boat that is easy to handle on the water and readily "forgives" your mistakes, or one that demands a high degree of skill? If you want to enjoy your new boat from the first stroke, get one that you can manage with the skills you have. Since it takes time to learn to scull well, make the time as enjoyable as you can. The pleasure of owning an expensive racing shell fades rapidly when you realize that you can't feel safe or comfortable in it. If you rush to acquire one before you are ready for it, every stroke you take will be shaped by the apprehension that you may roll over. Choose a boat that will permit you to scull with perfect confidence, a boat that will allow you to experiment with your blades, to take the risks that learning to scull well demands, in other words, a wherry or a similar relatively stable boat. When you are ready for a true racing shell, look for one that is suitable for your size and weight.

A 125-pound woman lifting a 30-pound boat lifts 24% of her weight; a 200-pound man lifting the same boat lifts 15% of his weight! Since singles weighing significantly less than 30 pounds are rare, small women find themselves at a disadvantage.

Durability is much more important to the large sculler than to the small one. The stresses he imposes on the boat significantly shorten the life of the boat. The right boat for you may not be the lightest boat you can buy, but a slightly heavier boat that will stand up to hard use. The two or three added pounds of weight make for a sturdier boat and represent a tiny fraction of your weight in combination with that of the boat.

In racing shell design, form follows function; decorative detail is minimal and unimportant. Form is dictated by:

- the need to minimize resistance caused by the hull's wave-making characteristics,

- the need to minimize skin friction,
- the need to support the weight of the sculler,
- the need to accommodate the dimensions of the sculler,
- the need to resist pitching as the sculler's weight moves
back and forth.

The wave-making capacity of the hulls of racing shells differs very slightly one from another. The useful limits of width and length have been exhaustively explored. A narrower boat may be faster, but is more unstable and harder to row, and may not adequately accommodate its crews. A wider boat may make it possible for a crew to perform better.

However, the shape of the boat accounts for less than ten percent of the resistance it creates by wave-making, so subtle alterations in shape do little more than identify a particular builder.

The greatest deterrent to the boat's progress is the friction between the boat's skin and the water. It accounts for nearly 90% of the total resistance. For this reason the cross-sections of all racing boats approach a semi-circular shape, which provides the greatest displacement and the least wetted surface. You can do much by your own efforts to reduce skin friction: keep your boat clean, free from blemishes, and polished.

The sea-keeping capacity of a boat depends on its ability to carry the weight of the sculler. It must have sufficient displacement to carry him on its proper waterline. If his weight sinks it too deep in the water, the added wetted surface increases skin friction. An overloaded boat will also take water over the deck, adding resistance and weight.

There are two principal dimensions in the design of a boat that relate directly to the proportions of the sculler. Although a given boat may adequately support a sculler, particularly a large one, the depth of the hull limits the distance between the sculler's seat and his heels. If this distance is curtailed by a shallow hull, he cannot reach well. For this reason he should check this dimension. Raising the seat to compensate an inadequate seat-above-heels distance will raise the sculler's center of gravity, decreasing the boat's stability. The other dimension is the length of the sculler's "stateroom," that is, the part of the boat that accommodates his legs in addition to his slide. For example, a large man's stateroom needs to be upwards of 54 inches long; a small woman's need only be 45 inches long. The shorter stateroom makes possible a shorter boat; a shorter, smaller boat makes the small sculler's work easier.

SEAT ABOVE HEELS

The forward and backward movement of the sculler causes the boat to pitch. To take care of this shifting load, builders design a little fullness near the ends of a racing shell. As a rule, the curves of the deck will show this fullness. Sometimes it appears in the profile of the boat where the line of the keel turns upward near the bow and stern.

The sliding rigger, a device that has periodically appeared on the rowing scene for a century or more, is designed to keep the rower's weight fixed in the boat, in order to minimize pitching. However, two years after it was used by a German sculler at Henley in 1981, the Fédération Internationale des Sociétés d' Avion (FISA) decided against its continued use in international rowing. They reasoned that it essentially redefined the sport and, further, that its acceptance would impose undue hardship on all but the wealthiest rowing organization.

BOAT FURNITURE

CLOGS

Because running shoes have almost replaced clogs in boats, you might think they are necessary. They become so only for people who use exaggeratedly awkward means to row, or who have very stiff ankles, or both. If you can hunker down and keep your heels on the ground, your ankles are sufficiently flexible to be accommodated quite comfortably in clogs.

Clogs allow you to feel the slightest change of pressure between the lacings and your insteps, provided you haven't laced them too tightly. Their curved bases keep your feet from sliding and prevent you from catching off your toes. They are lighter than shoes and vastly more sanitary. In case of a capsize, your feet slide readily free. This is not the case with running shoes that require the attachment of a safety tiedown at the heels to permit the rower to yank his feet out.

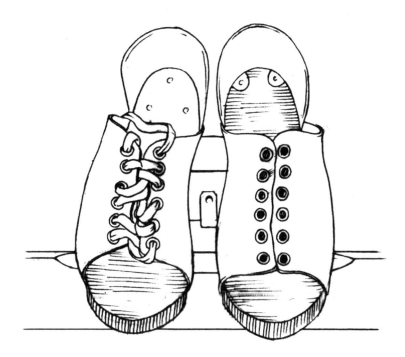

STRETCHERS

All stretchers are adjustable fore and aft; some can be adjusted for upward and downward placement of the clogs or shoes, and for the angle from the horizontal at which they can be set. Make sure that the range of adjustments to the stretcher suit your dimensions. The range of adjustment ought to be between 5 inches and 7 1/2 inches, measured from the lowest part of the heel cup or the shoe up to the lowest part of the seat. The angle of the footboard or clog ought to allow you to take the catch flat-footed. If you have flexible ankles this angle would be about 38 degrees from the horizontal. People who push with their toes are more comfortable if the footboard on which the shoes are mounted is angled more steeply than 38 degrees, say 42 or 43 degrees. This keeps their toes from being crowded in their shoes.

No builder today offers a stretcher fastening that is inherently difficult to comprehend, but many neglect to provide room enough for the hand that has to adjust them. And few builders now make a stretcher that is easy to repair. Spare parts are not available in hardware stores, nor are they easy to improvise.

SEATS

One of the first discoveries a beginner makes after half an hour in a racing shell is a passionate interest in a properly shaped seat. Although a good deal of thought has gone into their design, the seats that are provided in most boats are not custom-fitted. So, you may find one builder's seat more comfortable than another's simply because he has hit on a shape that suits you. George Pocock is credited with the idea of drilling holes in the depression of the modern seat to relieve pressure on the ischial tuberosities. Having rowed in the earlier version of a sliding seat, I can appreciate this innovation. Tried and discarded 90 years ago, another device for easing the rower's bottom was a wooden frame with leatherette stretched over it. The idea was that the surface of the seat would conform to the individual rower. However, it failed to solve the problem because the hard edges of the frame itself made the seat even more uncomfortable than the carved wooden seat.

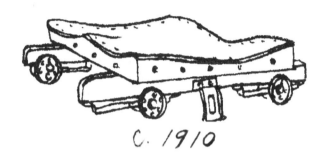

c. 1910

The spacing of the holes is critical because of the variations in male and female anatomy. If the bones are not settled in the middle of the holes, you won't be able to sit without pain for more than a minute. Recently, builders have taken to making oval holes that meet this necessity fairly successfully.

When you buy a boat, then, look for these holes and note their shape and spacing. Also, make sure that the edges of the holes are well rounded. Make sure that the edges of the seat are also softly rounded. This is especially important at the after-edge where pressure on the sciatic nerve can cause considerable distress. Carved wooden seats and molded plastic seats will incorporate these features more often than laminated wooden ones. The latter tend to be a good deal flatter, though, and for that reason are sometimes more comfortable for women.

You are going to spend a good many hours in your boat, so you should insist that the builder you purchase from provide you with a comfortable seat.

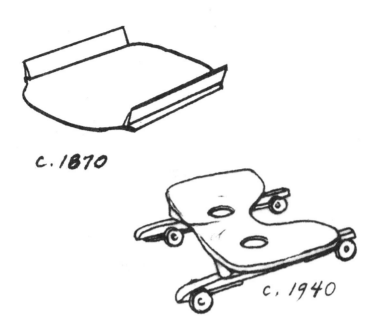

c. *1870*

c. *1940*

FIXED RIGGING

The earliest boats used for racing were provided with tholes, wooden dowels, set upright in pairs on the gunwales. (You might think that tholes are difficult to use, but they have been employed successfully since the dawn of rowing.) To maximize leverage the oarsmen sat across the thwarts or seats from the tholes. This made it possible to use a longer oar. As boats became narrower, this convention could not be counted on to produce the best leverage, so outriggers (since contracted to riggers) became necessary.

At first these outriggers simply displaced the tholes a short distance outward from their former position and a bit toward the bow. Later, as boats were made with less and less freeboard, that is, lower, in order to save weight, the riggers raised the tholes. Riggers became longer and lighter. The rigger length became standardized when the boats achieved minimal breadth.

ADJUSTABLE RIGGING
In recent years doubts about their dimensions have
prompted the development of completely adjustable riggers,
a decidedly mixed blessing. Adjusting the dimension of
one part of the rigging frequently requires changing all the
rest. The addition of joints and hold-fast devices impairs the
integrity of the rigger. Since there are frequently alternative
ways of adjusting some dimensions, like adjustable-pitch
rowlocks and extra-length thole pins with snap-on spacers for
changing rowlock heights, other rigger adjustments have been
made redundant. Look for the rigging that meets your physical
requirements with the least number of movable parts.

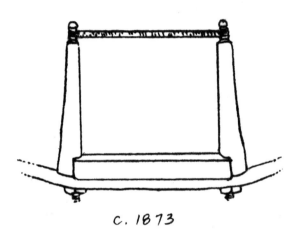

c. 1873

Modern plastic materials have made possible a light, strong,
wing-like frame that sits above the hull. This frame offers no
resistance to the water, has an airfoil shape and eliminates a
few of the compression and torsion forces imposed on the hull
by conventional riggers. It is more difficult to adjust for the
height of the rowlock, but that is a minor inconvenience that
can be remedied on some boats by the introduction of wedges
between the underside of the wing and its supports on the hull,
on others by the use of washers and longer bolts.

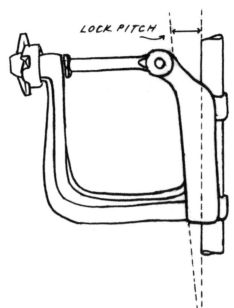

LOCK PITCH

ROWLOCKS

The swivel rowlock was an improvement on tholes. By confining the oar, it eliminates nearly all its unproductive motion. In modern rowlocks, pitch can be adjusted in several ways, according to the inventiveness of the manufacturer. Some rowlocks can be re-pitched in place, some must be removed from the post or thole pin. Durability, convenience, and subtlety of adjustment are given different priorities by each manufacturer.

A sometimes overlooked but important element in the design of a rowlock is the angle of the lower limb, the part that carries the oar on the feather. If you are rowing with pitched sculls, that is, fitted with wedges, the angle between the working face of the rowlock and the lower limb need only be about 90 degrees. For unpitched sculls such rowlocks are troublesome because they carry the blade at too small an angle to prevent it from crabbing. A better rowlock would have an angle of about 100 degrees.

THE GEOMETRY OF ROWING

THE SCULL'S MOST EFFECTIVE ARC

T he most effective portion of the arc would seem to lie 20 degrees either side of the rowline. Here, the vector AB, representing the force directed sternward by the blade, is much greater than the vector AC, representing the force directed at right angles to the boat. Add another 25 degrees to each side of the rowline and the vectors become equal. As much effort is apparently being used to move the water sideways as to propel the boat.

But it is a mistake to slight either end of the stroke just because it lies outside the middle 40-degree segment of the arc. It takes as much as 25 degrees to get the blade properly anchored, so that you can begin to pry the boat forward. It takes another 20 degrees to follow through, to produce the last increment of speed. Thus, the useful and necessary extent of the arc totals 85 degrees. The effectiveness of your stroke falls off rapidly if you cut it short at either end.

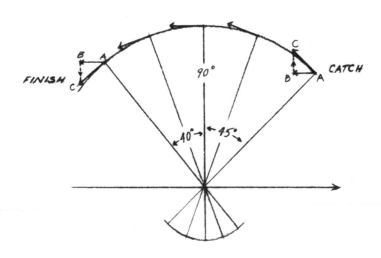

LOCATING THE ARC

To rig your boat so that you can achieve the arc universally accepted as the most effective, the first thing to do is to find the angles your sculls make with the rowline. For the purpose, draw a line across a piece of cardboard as in the illustration and place it next to the rowlock, so that the line is perpendicular to the centerline of the boat. Clip it or tape it to the rigger. At the dock with

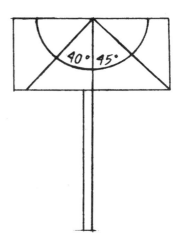

your sculls in place sit at the full reach and have someone slide a pencil along the loom to mark its position on the cardboard. Sit at the finish and repeat the process on the same side of the scull. Remove the cardboard and draw lines parallel to each of these lines such that they intersect the original line.

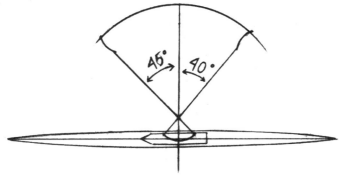

You may now measure the angles that your catch and finish make with the perpendicular. Compare them with the diagram to see if the arc of your stroke is distributed in the same way and extends as far.

Before going on to make any changes this comparison may suggest, check to see that your sculls are as close to your body at the finish as you can manage, the handles pointing at your backbone. If your handles pass by your body at a distance of several inches, move your stretcher aft until your handles just clear your body. Remember that your body will bend away from your handles at the finish of the stroke if you are pulling hard.

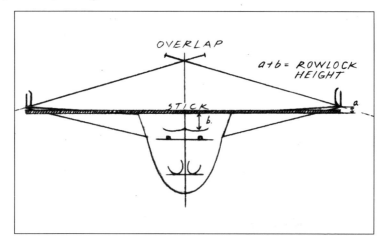

OVERLAP

Next, look at the amount of crossover your handles have at mid-stroke. The more overlap you can comfortably accommodate, the more leverage you can get from your sculls. Measure the width of your hand across the knuckles. Your overlap should be between one and two times this amount. If you find you have less overlap than this, relocate your collars outward. If you are a short person, this change may cause the handles to interfere with your body, since you may already have set your stretcher as far forward as it will go. Conversely, if you have too much overlap—more likely for a tall person using too much inboard—reduce the inboard dimension.

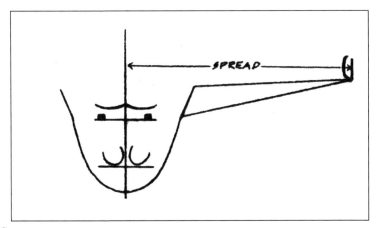

SPREAD

You can now adjust the spread. If you are tall, you may find it easy to swing through an arc of 85 degrees, perhaps even more. Move your collars out, and move your rowlocks out a corresponding amount, increasing the spread until the arc you row falls within 85 degrees. If you are short, move your collars and rowlocks in, reducing the spread until you can achieve the complete arc. This may not be possible for a person who is only 5'-4" tall, if the rigging cannot be altered to provide a short enough spread. However, after making these adjustments the tall person may now have too small a load and the short person too great. So, you should prepare to make a few calculations.

RATIO AND SCULL LENGTH

Ratio approximately defines load. It refers to the relation-ship between the outboard and the inboard length of your sculls: R = OL / IL. The proper ratio permits you to sustain appropriate stroke rates at race pace. A strong man over 6 feet tall, using standard 9'-10" (300 cm) sculls, might use a ratio of 2.40:1; an OL of 6'-11" (212 cm) and an IL of 2'-11" (88 cm). A small woman, whose upper body strength is not commensurate with a man's might opt to use sculls 9'-9"

(296 cm) long (a fairly common choice), and a ratio of 2.35:1; an OL of 6'–10" (208 cm), and an IL of 2'–11" (88 cm). However, although the ratio may be appropriate to her size and strength, a reasonable overlap of, say, 7" (18 cm) would require that her rigging be spread 5'–3" (159 cm). Obviously, her short stature will not allow her to achieve an arc of much over 65 degrees, far from ideal. She would be well advised to find a boat builder who can provide her with properly scaled equipment.

Exceptionally tall men (6'–8") must have longer sculls and spreads that are greater than the norm, unless they curtail their reach and use less slide in order to stay within the 85-degree arc.

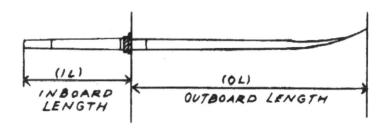

RIGGING FOR ROWING

With a few qualifications, all the foregoing applies to oars or sweeps. The rower's reach is less than the sculler's because it is defined by the extension of the "outside" arm. At the other end of the stroke, his handle crosses in front of his body. In order to complete the effective arc the rower must bring the end of the handle close to his body, but the handle should not extend past it. In order for the rower's handle to arrive at the appropriate place relative to his body, he must have the correct spread for the inboard length (IL) of his oar. The difference between IL and spread for large people is about a foot. For smaller people it should be as little as 9 inches. A large man, using a 12'–6" (381 cm) sweep might use a ratio of 2.38:1, an OL of 8'–10" (268 cm), and an IL of 3'–8" (113 cm). Given an IL less spread of no more than 12" (30 cm) spread should be set at 2'–8 (82 cm) measured to the bulge of the rowlock.

To enable a small woman to pull such an oar, 12'–6" (381 cm), the ratio would have to be lower, say 2.33:1. The OL would then be 8'–9" (267 cm), the IL 3'–9" (114 cm). The spread, IL less the same 12" (30 cm) as for the man, would then be 2'–9". However, the oar handle would extend past her body at the finish of the stroke, impairing her ability to keep pressure on it, and the arc of her stroke would be 15 to 20 degrees less than the optimum 85 degrees.

Quite plainly, a small woman should use a much smaller oar, and row a boat fitted with riggers short enough to enable her to achieve the most effective arc.

These numbers serve only for comparison. The actual lever represented by the oar or scull ought to be measured from the points at which force is applied at the handle and at the center of the area of the blade. The oar pivots not at the working face of the collar from which point the inboard and the outboard lengths are measured, but at a short distance outboard on the sleeve opposite the pin. The numbers do go to show, however, that in order to reproduce the optimum arc of the stroke for all classes and sizes of scullers and rowers, a number of significant measurements have to be manipulated.

BLADE PITCH
One variable that can easily be eliminated from the rigging process is blade pitch, simply by making it zero.

That is, correct any deviation between the flat bearing surface of the sleeve and the short axis of the blade. Place a short length of 2 x 4 crossways in the cup of the blade and holding this with the blade facing downward at eye level, sight back to another short straight bit of wood lying across the sleeve. Make sure the two pieces of wood lie at right angles to the centerline of the scull or oar, and look for divergence of the edges.

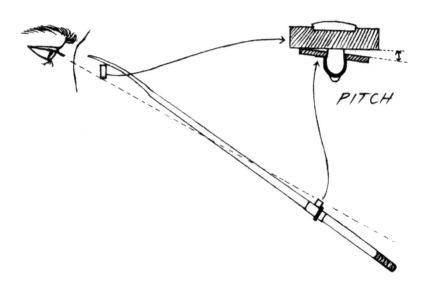

PITCH

If in a pair of wooden sculls you find a small deflection in each, but in the opposite direction, mark the sculls port and starboard so that the deflection adds pitch when the scull is in the rowlock. If the deflection is small enough, you can scrape or sand enough from the high edge of the sleeve to bring it to 0 degrees. If it is large, you can loosen the collar and slip a thin wooden wedge under the low corner.

The sleeves of carbon fiber sculls and oars can be trued

with a knife or rasp. They are made with high edges for that reason.

ROWLOCK PITCH
More important than the actual fore and aft pitch of the rowlocks is that it be the same in both rowlocks. The simplest and the most reliable way to check for this is to clamp a stick against the face of each rowlock. Swing the rowlocks parallel to the center line of the boat and sight across the boat from one stick to the other. If the sticks aren't parallel, adjust the rowlock with less pitch until it agrees with the other. (Pitch meters that depend on a bubble are less likely to produce parallelism than the stick method.)
The amount of pitch to use, as a rule of thumb, should diminish as you gain experience. Eight or nine degrees suffice for the beginner, as few as four degrees for the adept. For a club single six degrees will be quite suitable.
   Outboard pitch is usually built into the rigger. It should be between 1 degree and 1–1/2 degrees. Outboard pitch adds blade pitch at the catch to keep the blade from going deep, reduces it at the finish making it easier to keep the blade covered. If adjustment is available, keep within the above range.

ROWLOCK HEIGHT
You should set your rowlocks at a height above the seat that will allow comfortable and efficient working of the sculls. What other scullers choose offers only the roughest of guides. As your dexterity improves you will find that you need less height to achieve both efficiency and comfort.
   Efficiency demands that the blades remain locked in the water as long as possible. If you find it difficult to keep your blades covered, you are probably rigged too high. Comfort dictates that you be able to clear your thighs easily as you bring your blades back on the recovery. If you cannot, you are

probably rigged too low.

Rowlock height is measured from the lowest portion of the seat (the edge of the holes) to the mid-point of the lower limb of the rowlock. It varies between 3–1/2 inches for the smallest sculler to 7 inches for the largest—as a rule. Few boats, if any, allow for such a range, so some improvisation may be necessary. It is possible to learn to scull with your rowlocks at even heights, but you will be more comfortable rowing left over right with your starboard rowlock a quarter inch to a half inch higher than your port.

To measure rowlock height place a straight stick across the top edges of the gunwales square to the center line with one end under the rowlock. Measure from the top of each track to the bottom edge of the stick to see if the stick is parallel to the rower's bench. If it is not, place spacers between the stick and the appropriate edge of the boat to bring the stick parallel. Measure from the seat up to the stick and add that amount to the measurement from the bottom of the stick to the mid-point of the rowlock.

Builders of both racing and recreational sliding seat boats nowadays set the rowlocks and riggers high, six inches or more above the seat. This provides good accommodation for very large scullers, beginners and scullers who turn their sculls with their wrists. It also allows moving the seat out of the bow at the same time as the hands at the completion of the stroke. Scullers who learn the proper hold do not need extra room for their wrists under the handle, nor do they need the high rigging necessitated by bringing the knees up under the hands on the recovery.

SCALING AND FITTING EQUIPMENT
With the re-emergence of women's rowing in the early sixties, the need for appropriately sized equipment became apparent. Only very recently, however, have boat and equip-

ment manufacturers begun to meet that need. Even so, since so much rowing equipment must be shared, ways have to be found to provide women with the sort of boats and oars that permit them to row as efficiently and comfortably as men do with equipment designed for men. Virtually everything is too big for women. However, anyone who has a modicum of skill and the willingness to try can modify this equipment.

MODIFICATIONS TO SCULLS
WOODEN SCULLS

A small woman weighing, say, 115 pounds should have sculls no longer than 9'–5" (287 cm) and more flexible than sculls used by bigger people. If sculls of that length aren't readily available, they can be made by modifying a longer set.

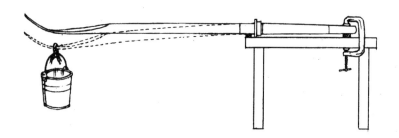

Before cutting down the sculls, find out how flexible they are. Provide a jig as suggested by the illustration and support one of the sculls so that measurements can be taken from the tip of the blade to the floor before and after a ten- to fifteen-pound weight is suspended from the blade.

Next, cut the scull to the suggested length and re-shape the handle as in the drawing, reducing its diameter to about 1–1/8 inches.

Plane down the sides of the scull a little at a time as in the illustration, returning it to the jig at intervals to see how much flexibility it has gained. Continue this process until the deflection of the scull is about 15 percent more than it had originally.

Lastly, reduce the width of the blade by cutting the edges back 3/8 inch to 1/2 inch at the widest part, and tapering to the tip and the throat.

CARBON FIBER SCULLS

Carbon fiber sculls have either wooden or plastic handles. You can cut up to 1–1/4 inch off the ends because they are over 5–1/4 inches long, more than long enough for the largest hand. To make a shorter scull, cut 3 inches off the shaft (the plug is not quite 3 inches long), clean and slightly taper the plug and reset it with epoxy glue. Aim for a snug fit. Reset the sleeve nearer the blade.

To get more flexibility in the scull, trim the loom from the sleeve to the blade, by grinding on the side opposite the flat part of the sleeve, feathering the sanding as you near the sleeve and the blade. Be careful. The wall of the loom is thin. Test the flexibility before you make any changes in the scull and retest until you have reached an increase of 10 to 15 percent.

Use a hacksaw or a grinder to cut back the edges of the blades to produce a flatter curve, leaving the full width at the end of the blade. Although the core material is impervious to water, it is a good idea to seal the newly cut edges with epoxy glue or putty to keep them from becoming ragged.

WOODEN SWEEPS

Wooden sweeps can be shortened about 6" (15 cm) by sawing off the handle. Because they are hollow throughout most of the loom below the sleeve, shortening them further brings the hollow part to the fulcrum, and makes the oar susceptible to failure.

Shave the looms in the same way as for sculls, taking wood from the sides and trimming back the edges of the hardwood compression strip usually found on the flat side of the oar. Test them for bending in the same way as for sculls. Cut about 3/8 inch from each edge to reduce the area of the blades.

CARBON FIBER SWEEPS

Carbon fiber oars are fitted with extremely long wooden handles so that up to 5 inches can be cut off the ends without forcing the oarsman to grasp the carbon fiber shaft of the oar. You can also cut 4 inches from the carbon fiber shaft, re-taper the plug and re-set it in epoxy glue. This method allows you to cut the oar as short as you like.

You should remove laminate from the side of the oar opposite the flat side of the collar just as for sculls, because the oar is going to gain stiffness as it is shortened. The process is laborious, especially if you try to preserve the roundness of the shaft. An appropriately flexible oar is more efficient and prevents injury.

HEIGHT OF WORK

Women, rowing in boats too large for them, have to pull their handles back high, and finish in a weak and awkward position. Padding their seats with some sort of cushion rarely gets them high enough.

A better way is to separate the seat top from the horns that carry the wheels, by introducing between them a spacer or lift of up to an inch of thickness.

SEAT ABOVE HEELS

A sculler with long legs and a short torso may need more seat-above-heels height than his boat can accommodate in order to achieve a comfortable reach position. The only way to increase the seat-above-heels dimension is to raise the seat by the method previously described or by placing battens under the tracks. Although either method makes a tippy boat tippier, it is still worth doing for the comfort it provides.

CLOG AND SHOE SETTINGS

If clogs appropriate for women are not fitted in a boat, heel cups fastened to wedges can be inserted into men's clogs. They may be fastened in or carried in and out of the boat. The rowers' feet will keep them in place.

They have several purposes: to reduce the seat-above-heels dimension; to reduce the interference of the after-ends of the tracks and rower's bench with the rower's calves; to lessen the angle through which the ankle has to bend; and to accommodate rowers with stiff ankles or short Achilles tendons.

Where shoes are fitted to the stretcher, alternative upward and downward settings are usually provided. But where there are not enough settings, the shoes may have to be mounted on a metal plate, dimensioned and drilled to allow adjustment.

NON-BOAT EQUIPMENT

CAR-TOPPING BOATS

Road-tripping rowers need to be able to tie boats securely to car tops. There is a simple method to doing this to wherries, singles and doubles and other smaller craft with an economy of rope and macrame. (Check your state's department of motor vehicles for length limitations.)

If you tie your boat directly to the car top, be sure to pad the roof with foam or towelling. If it is practical, tie through the interior structure of the boat rather than around the hull. This is fine for short distances at moderate speeds.

You may be travelling on the freeway or in windy areas, or going a long way, or perhaps be carrying more than one boat. You will want to arrest sliding and bouncing by stabilizing the ends of the boat. This can be done very quickly with nylon rope and a bit of padding. To do this:

◆ Place a pad on top of your car. Unrig your boat and put it upside down on top of your car, centering the weight of the boat.

◆ Tie a loop on one end of a rope about 20 feet long. Slide it securely over the right side of the front bumper. Throw the loose end of the rope over the boat, and wrap it once around the existing rope. Don't knot anything. The bracing must be able to slide and self-adjust in order to work as a system. If the boat is particularly fragile, put a bit of padding between the rope and the boat's skin.

◆ To make a Trucker's Hitch, tie a small leverage loop in the rope about two feet above the left front bumper.

◆ Run the loose end of the rope around the left side of the bumper so it is snug but not tight, and thread it back through the leverage loop.

◆ Pull the rope downward, using the loop as a pulley. Secure the rope with a half hitch for now.

◆ Do steps 2–5 to the rear bumper, and tighten, finishing with several half hitches.

◆ Go to the front bumper and re-tighten the fastening. Neither end of the boat should move in any direction, but don't overdo it so that the rope stresses the boat with normal car vibrations. Secure red flagging on the end of the boat.

BUILDING A BOAT CRADLE
If you plan to move your boat more than a few miles,
you should carry it in a boat cradle.

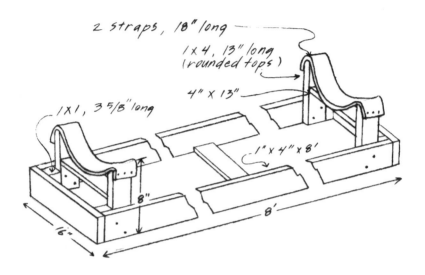

BOAT STORAGE
It is not always possible to store a boat inside, where it will
be protected from the elements. Plastic boats are vulnerable
to sun, wooden boats to both sun and rain. No boat should
be wrapped in fitted covers that prevent the circulation of
air. Metal parts corrode and rust, wooden parts mildew and
rot. A simple shed without walls will do if it keeps boats out
of the sun and rain. Locate it, if possible, on the north side
of an existing structure.

Any ports or bungs fitted to boats made wholly or partly
of wood should be opened before storage to allow the circulation of air through the length of the boat. Be sure that all
surfaces are dry and, when exposed to salt water, rinsed with fresh
water and dried. Near salt water the air is also salty so metal
parts ought to be greased lightly and checked periodically.

ROWING IN FACSIMILE

Rowing ergometers have their uses. You can get lots of exercise on them. Some have devices for quantifying your efforts. By using one machine as a standard, you can compare the energy output of athletes, one with another, as well as to measure individual progress in strength and endurance.

But rowing ergometers are a poor substitute for rowing in a boat. Furthermore, they obscure the degree of skill that is necessary to be a competent sculler. Mole and Water Rat may be able to clarify my reasons for thinking so. (Mole and Water Rat are characters from Kenneth Grahame's *The Wind in the Willows*.)

MOLE AND WATER RAT
DISCUSS THE ERGOMETER

Mole stood awhile watching a pair of novices put their wherries in the water and with some difficulty scrabble their way clear of the dock. He listened to Water Rat's quiet instructions to the pair and hoped that one day he himself could attain the lore, the command of language and the patience of Water Rat. When the novices were safely on their way, he approached Water Rat diffidently, cleared his throat and blurted, "I have an ergometer."

Water Rat turned toward his young friend with an indulgent smile and said, "Have you now?"

Mole: Yes, and I want to know whether I can learn to row as well as exercise on it.

Water Rat: Why ever not?

Mole: Of course, there's no water.

Water Rat: Well, you would need something that at least

	works like an oar.
Mole:	My ergometer doesn't have an oar, just a bit of dowel you hang onto.
Water Rat:	Can you turn the dowel?
Mole:	No. It doesn't turn; it's just this round thing hitched to a bicycle chain.
Water Rat:	Then I think we ought to look for a way to make this dowel rotate to imitate the turning of the oar.
Mole:	Is that necessary? There's a seat that goes back and forth just like the one in a boat.
Water Rat:	But you must join the working of the fingers to the movement of the slide. There's a little flick you give the handle every time you change direction on the slide. Maybe, if a metal rod were substituted for the wooden dowel and handles made for it that would rotate...
Mole:	That shouldn't be too difficult, but I still don't see why it is so important.
Water Rat:	Simple. If you don't train your fingers to react to changes of direction in the slide, it is too easy to fall into the habit of turning the oar with your wrist when you get into a boat. By the way, is this ergometer you are telling me about really made for learning how to row?
Mole:	I think so. Well, I don't know. All I know is, you pull on the handle as hard as you can and this little needle swings around.
Water Rat:	And that tells you how hard you are pulling?
Mole:	Yes.
Water Rat:	Anything else? Like whether you can be sure that what you are doing will move a boat?
Mole:	I don't know. I'm not sure.
Water Rat:	Exactly. It would help, I think, to cut off the little jigger with the needle and the dial.

	Perhaps you can use it on your bicycle.
Mole:	Why take off the dial with the needle?
Water Rat:	Well, what do you want to find out? How fast you can make the wheel go 'round, or how to row better? With that little dial you can fool yourself into thinking you are learning to row better, if you can make it give you a high score.
Mole:	I guess I could get along without it. Then would my ergometer help my rowing?
Water Rat:	Not quite, but we've made a good start. You need a mirror, of course, mounted on casters so you can see yourself from the front and from the side.
Mole:	Why should I want to see myself?
Water Rat:	To help you to get into position properly. It's not always easy to tell when you've got it right without an observer or a mirror. For instance, if you are trying to learn how to lengthen your back to improve your reach, it helps to be able to see where it bends. The less bend, of course, the better; the reach comes from the hips.
Mole:	I'm beginning to wonder if maybe...
Water Rat:	Wait a minute. There is one more thing.
Mole:	*Yes?* What is that?
Water Rat:	Does your ergometer have wheels on it?
Mole:	Of course not.
Water Rat:	You know that every move you make in a boat causes it to move in the opposite direction. That's because it is supported in a medium that offers very little resistance.
Mole:	So what does that have to do with my ergometer?
Water Rat:	Don't you think you ought to get used to trying to avoid shoving the boat in the wrong direction? With wheels on your ergometer

	you could reproduce this effect.
Mole:	But I thought you said I could learn to row on my ergometer, I mean, the way it is now.
Water Rat:	I was wrong.

◆MASTERY◆
LEARNING STRATEGIES

LOOKING AT FILMS AND TAPES

The increasing availability of films and tapes of the best scullers and rowers has made it possible to study them conveniently. Keep in mind that you may have to make allowances for lapses from form caused by the intensity of their efforts. You should try to discern the difference between what the athlete is doing and what he is *trying* to do. Try to imagine what he might look like when he is not pushed to the breaking point.

A few examples may help you.

The great Romanian sculler, Valeria Racila—driving toward the finish line, passing her last rival— knees bobbing up just before the finish of the stroke, her legs no longer able to force the stroke home.

The Hansen brothers of Norway, in spite of blades breaking loose at the finish, beating a superb Russian double in the last fifty meters simply because the Russians have been unable to maintain the pace.

A New Zealand eight winning the World Championships in 1983 with four collapsing toward his handle at the finish of each stroke and number six finishing early. Neither man has any intention of quitting, but the cadence has become virtually beyond their strength.

What you see at the finish of a boat race is what is left of technique after it has been eroded by strenuous exertion and excitement, to say nothing of the deterrent effect of wind and water.

CHAMPIONS AND THEIR QUIRKS
Idiosyncrasy characterizes a good deal of rowing, as it does other sports, even among the very best. But where champions

transcend their little quirks, the folks at the other end of the spectrum, who may mistake these foibles for the keys to mastery, are doomed to disappointment. Try to imitate a given athlete, the exact curve of his back, for example. How does that particular shape serve him better than another? Would it serve you as well? Or imitate the positioning of his hands on the sculls. Does it explain the dexterity of his bladework? Would his method work for you? A few examples will show you what I mean.

Al Shealy, the great Harvard stroke of 1973–1975, liked to give his arms a little shake just before he dropped his blade in the water. When he was rowing on the national team in 1976, his coach, Al Rosenberg, tried unsuccessfully to get him to stop doing it. Only Shealy knew why he did it, but I suspect it kept his arms loose and helped him reach out. Possibly a good idea, but I have never known anyone to imitate it.

At the world championships in Nottingham, England in 1975 many coaches there were much taken with the East German pair, two brothers, and decided to shape their instruction on the example of this very successful crew. The brothers were unique in several ways. They took the water with their inside wrists strongly arched. This permitted them to clear the oar with a flat wrist and consequently to row with a lower rig than would have been the case had they let their wrists fall under the handle. They also rowed with their backs bowed to the limit and looked, to say the least, uncomfortable. Coaches generally seem to have ignored the peculiarity of the wrist action, but approved of the bent backs, even though for these particular oarsmen it was simply easier to reach from the middle of their backs than from their hips.

It goes without saying that to force this model on women would be particularly harmful. Yet, many coaches direct women to row with bent backs, not because it achieves a longer reach but because it looks better to them, that is, like many men whose lack of hip mobility prevents them from achieving the reach in any other way.

All of the eye-catching peculiarities of technique in these world class athletes can divert attention from the true indicators of their skill and mastery: the clean bladework and seamless movement that transcends their idiosyncrasies.

Chris Penny, who rowed on the 1984 Olympic eight, had the busiest hands I have ever seen. They were like the hands of a card sharp. He repositioned his feathering hand a good 60 degrees in two directions every time he came down the slide, and did it so quickly the hand was just a blur. The merit of this fast shuffle was that it made it impossible to grip the handle. I'm sure he thought no more about it than he did about brushing his teeth. The gesture had long ago passed from the conscious to the unconscious part of his brain.

Christine Scheiblich, world champion from 1974 through 1978 lifted her elbows to release her blades. Why? Was it necessary? Was she fast because of this idiosyncrasy, or in spite of it? I never learned, but I suspect that it was a carryover from her first year of sculling.

TAKING INSTRUCTION

When Benny Goodman decided to learn how to play the classical clarinet, he was already a world-renowned musician with a perfected technique, acquired from years of playing popular music. His teacher asked him to cut the calluses off his fingers. In order to learn the touch of a classical clarinetist he had to become a beginner again. Had he not been willing to sensitize his fingers he would have found himself depending on instruction alone. This, his teacher insisted, would not be enough.

Whether you are just starting out or looking for ways to improve your sculling, you may find yourself in a position much like Benny Goodman's. Be prepared to learn good sculling through touch and hearing. Simply doing what you are asked, literal-mindedly, fragments the stroke. "Connecting the dots" will not bring you to the essence of the sculler's art. Rather, it will make you victim to fallacies, misconceptions, aberrations and delusions, like the following.

THE SCULLER'S CHOKE

Asked to curl their thumbs around the ends of their handles, many scullers grasp their handles an inch or so from the end, forcing their thumbs to reach around it. This hold sacrifices an inch or more of leverage and virtually

guarantees that they will use their wrists to turn the scull. This hold works better on a garden hose when you don't have a nozzle and want to create a strong jet or fine spray.

THE FLAT WRIST

Many scullers try to keep their wrists flat throughout the drive or pull-through. To accomplish this they have to flare their elbows as they complete the stroke. Flaring the elbows drastically reduces the effectiveness of the arms and shoulders at the finish. It also imposes unnecessary strains on the tendon running through the tops of their wrists. Concentrate on pulling with your shoulders, squeezing them together at the finish of the stroke, and your elbows will fall to your sides and your wrists will take a natural arch. You will pull more effectively and avoid injury.

BACKSPLASH
Backsplash refers to the water struck off the back of the blade on its way toward the bow, incidental to the recovery. It occurs when the blade is rolled up too soon, allowing the trailing edge to strike the water before the sculler has achieved his full reach.

The fallacy is in thinking that one should *try* to produce back splash, the sure indication that the blade is ready to be pulled into the water. From this misconception, it is easy to conclude that one should drop the blade in the water, and then pull.

The sculler and oarsman should carry the blade on the feather as long as possible, so that it squares *as it enters the water*, propelled by the rower's full weight. The blade has to be driven in at maximum speed because the water it is entering is passing the boat so rapidly. The perfect entry produces a small splash from both sides of the blade.

THE HARD CATCH
A look of grim determination combined with a quick lift of the back and a toss of the head usually signal the Hard Catch. To maximize the force they can deliver to the sculls, scullers will swing their blades off the water as they reach out so that they can deliver a blow that jolts their shoulders and backs. Their sculls bend to their limits.

But what is happening while their blades are on their way into the water? Their torsos are moving rapidly toward the bow. The consequence is that the boat, being only one-fifth the weight of the crew or less, is thrust rapidly sternward, and continues to do so until blades are solidly anchored. So, the satisfying impact these athletes are experiencing does not produce speed. Because their bodies are moving forward, they assume that they are moving the boat forward. In fact, they are pushing the boat backward until they are well into the stroke.

The relief scullers experience when they substitute the Sculler's Catch for the Hard Catch is second only to the joy of discovering that they are going faster. The superior, quick, catch is achieved with a very light touch on the handles and a leap from the stretcher. The stroke begins with an instantaneous change of direction: the blade engages the water as it goes by.

THE SQUARED RELEASE
It is a common belief that the blade should leave the water "squared." You may see crews performing the "square blade drill," sometimes for miles. And it is a pretty difficult drill. Undeniably, it requires some real application to the matter of balancing the boat. Since a squared blade presents a sometimes abrupt deterrent to progress if it touches the water on its way forward, every rower is at some pains to keep this from happening. The result is that the blade is carried higher than would be necessary were it feathered. But it virtually guarantees a washed-out finish, particularly as the rate goes up.

Since you grasp the handles of sculls and oars from the top, you impart some torque to them. Rowlocks are pitched to resist this torque. Oars, in fact, want to ride not on the flat of the back of the sleeve, but on the upper corner, as explained earlier, so that in the square blade drill you must make a determined effort to keep the oar blades squared over as you approach the finish of the stroke. If fatigue overcomes you and you let the blade out a little early, you wash out. However, quite unconsciously, you may let your sculls roll a little in your fingers and discover that the blade stays in the water without effort.

But what if you sought a way to extract your blades as quickly as possible and yet carry the strongest propulsive effect to the very moment of extraction? By inclining your blades at the approach of the release, you make sure that they can not wash out. The wedging effect of your blades forces them down, bending your oar very slightly downward. You do not have to pull the handle upward to keep the blade buried; you need only *let* the handle rise until you strike the handle away, while the looms are still bent. The result: your blades release cleanly, to be feathered as they leave the water when you roll your handles in your fingers.

THE KNEE BOB
The knee bob occurs when the legs, driving the seat forward, straighten, then flex upward again. It is always preceded by a slump in the lower back, which, in turn may be caused by sitting on the tailbone rather than the hams. The knee bob signals a loss of pressure at the finish of the stroke, something to avoid at all costs. Concentrate on holding both knees down until your hands clear your knees in order to guarantee a solid finish.

THE PINKY LOCK
One anomaly of sweep rowing is to let the little finger of the outside hand hang over the end of the handle, perhaps to maximize leverage. But it can be a dangerous thing to do, as anyone who has let his handle drop below the edge of the coaming and jammed his little finger against the shoulder knows. But even though that problem has been virtually eliminated in many modern racing shells, dropping the little finger over the end of the handle moves the hand away from the body at the

finish of the stroke, lessening the effectiveness of that arm and shoulder.

CATCHING OFF THE TOES
I was coaching a pretty fair high school four of mine one day when my eye was caught by a sudden sharp rise of the two man's knees just as he entered the water. I had never seen that movement before, and I did not immediately tumble to the reason for it. I let the crew row on for half a mile or so and, when I thought the time had come to deal with this aberration, I stopped them. I asked number two how he was producing this interesting, and for me, distracting effect. He explained that he had learned from his brother, a university oarsman, how to shove off his toes.

"Don't your calves get tired?" I asked.

"Just a little," he replied.

"Can you complete your reach without lifting your heels?"

"Yes."

The dialogue that followed was mercifully short; the gist of it was that if you weren't compelled by stiff ankles or a footboard too steeply pitched to catch off your toes, you should do your work by pressing with your whole foot. You will then make no extraneous movements and be a lot more stable in your boat.

THE ONE-HANDED CATCH
In a desperate attempt to increase his reach a rower will often slide his outside hand down the handle, or let go of it altogether. At the moment of the catch the rower has in the first instance lost a few valuable inches of leverage. In the second instance all the work of the catch is done by his inside hand, while the outside hand

135

hovers uselessly above the handle. The rower who is thinking of reaching as far as he can from his hips will not make this mistake.

WINGING ELBOWS
The raising of the outside elbow at the end of the pull-through will betray the rower who uses his lockside arm to complete the stroke. His outside hand may slide across the top of his handle, making a straight line from his fingertips to his elbow. The consequence is a quick drop in pressure on the blade, making it necessary for him to jerk the blade out of the water. The leverage advantage of the outside shoulder and arm is wasted.

If a rower is using both arms and shoulders properly, his elbows cannot rise. This is easily demonstrated on an ergometer, in particular the kind that makes use of a vaned wheel for resistance. If another person holds the wheel when the rower begins to pull the handle, letting it rotate very slowly under his hands, the rower will complete the stroke with his elbows below the level of his hands.

To test whether letting the elbows rise at the end of the stroke is equally effective, the rower should next attempt to complete the stroke with his elbows held at the level of his hands. His partner, as before, keeps the wheel rotating slowly. As this handle approaches his chest the rower will discover that he simply cannot maintain full pressure on his handle. His partner will have little difficulty keeping the wheel from rotating.

THE SLOW SLIDE
The object of the Slow Slide is to return the rower to his full reach position in time to make the catch, but no sooner. However, the effort to achieve a slow slide leads to two errors: first, a slowing down or hesitation at about half-slide;

and second, a shortening of the stroke at both ends as the rate goes up. In both instances, the sculler's commitment to the *idea* of a slow slide forces him to give it undue importance. Since you have to swing your body back through the same arc described by the pull-through, it is easy to believe that by slowing this movement you are slowing the slide. But slide motion is produced by the bending of the legs. If you delay the body swing and the return of the handles, you are putting off the moment when you can start down the slide. Time is wasted, and your weight settles in the bow of the boat.

THE LONG SLIDE
The long slide has replaced the traditional twenty-seven inch slide and is up to six inches longer. What is not clearly understood is the reason for it. The rationalization — as distinct from the reason — is that the extra length, extended sternward, permits the rower to reach farther and to achieve greater compression of the legs, hence, more leg drive. The argument goes this way: the legs are the strongest element in the total anatomy, strong legs make strong rowers, longer slides equate with longer strokes.

Bringing his buttocks farther aft rounds the rower's lower back, making it vulnerable to excessive strain and injury, especially if this position is unnatural to him. For such athletes to pull their buttocks under them is to risk injury and to impair their ability to apply maximum pressure to the oar. The reason for this position is easier to understand when you realize that a great many men have difficulty reaching from the hips. Because of their limited mobility, they are forced to round their backs.

For people who have been trained to elongate their backs from their hips, or who do it naturally and easily—and this includes most women—reaching is easy. For them the necessity for the long slide doesn't exist.

The foregoing errors result as a rule from the athlete's intense desire to master the art of sculling or rowing. Simply put, he tries too hard, so much of his effort is misdirected. In each instance above, a slight change in the way he goes about his work will make it easier and more efficient. I must add parenthetically that it is not unusual for an athlete to have misgivings about a modification of his technique that has eased his burden. For this athlete, inconvenience and painful effort have come to define the sport. So, avoid anomalies like the foregoing by focussing on the essential stroke which is symmetrical, spontaneous, apparently effortless and perfectly economical.

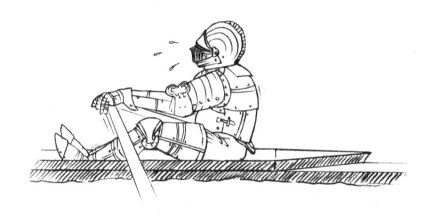

FOUR SCULLERS

The following four scullers were subject to the same caprices and impediments that get in the way of any dedicated sculler. In time, through perseverance and faith, they pushed past them and achieved for themselves a good deal of satisfaction and a measure of fame. They are outstanding examples of athletes who went about learning to scull, painstakingly and joyfully.

CECILY COUGHLAN

I began a correspondence with Cecily while she was completing her studies at Brown University and thinking of becoming a sculler. Although she weighed only 115 pounds, she had stroked her JV crew. I attempted to answer her questions and to encourage her to be her own coach. She tested my suggestions extensively on the water and made some valuable discoveries.

One that she found quite useful came out of her efforts to avoid scraped knuckles. She had to learn how to keep her hands one before the other. She tried leading the same hand on pull-through and recovery, and switching hands. She settled finally on leading the same hand both on pull-through and recovery. To keep her left hand farther away than her right, "I finally just imagined that one arm was shorter than the other," she wrote. She was then able to pull her handles through, one behind the other, consistently.

Another discovery followed my suggestion that she stop trying to reach with a bent back and instead reach from her hips. By bending her back, she had been straining it. "It feels like I come out of a curl and reach across the deck to the catch, straightening out the line of my spine in the process. When I feel this swing I also find that my hips travel a different rate from my hands and shoulders into the stern. It's almost a matter of pressing my belly down as I reach across the water."

With this discovery she began to realize that the beginning of the stroke must be made *while* the lower back is being drawn down. This is important. The muscles that straighten out the lower back have to be tense to the instant of the catch.

By this time she had reached the limit of what she could accomplish with equipment ill-suited to her size.

When we met in Seattle, Cecily was surprised and pleased to find out that, with smaller sculls, 9'–5" rather than 9'–8" in length, and blades narrowed about half an inch; a much lower rig, 4–1/2" off the seat rather than 6 inches; and reduced spread, 60 inches rather than 64 inches, she could lower her stroke rate and go faster.

One final discovery came when we set out to find a remedy for the chronic problem she was having with one of her ribs. Rowing bow to her stroke in a double one day, I noticed that a point midway on her back moved sideways about 3/8 of an inch, when she began each stroke. I asked her to hold it straight, but that seemed to make it worse. It certainly didn't make it better. She tried pushing harder on one foot. Still no improvement. She pushed harder on the other foot. Immediately, her back straightened, and it remained straight throughout every stroke thereafter, so long as she emphasized the push on that foot.

At that point I thought to ask her which rib was causing the pain and whether she felt any pain now. She traced the rib back to her spine, to the exact spot that I had seen move. The pain had been caused whenever she had applied enough force to dislodge the rib, that is, whenever she rowed hard. We continued to row, but after a dozen strokes she said that her leg was tiring. We could only conclude that she had spent a good many years rowing one-legged! Some months after the day in question, she told me that she had been kicked in the sternum by a horse when she was eight years old. The memory suddenly surfaced while she was being treated by her Rolfer friend Sherri Cassuto.

Lots of people row one-legged, but since they have no vulnerable spots in their backs they escape injury. Still, they may strain their backs from time to time, unless they can learn to row with symmetry, and backs properly aligned. Equal pressure should be easy to achieve in a single, but Cecily had done most of her rowing in an eight, and formed habits that she brought with her to sculling. When she learned to use her legs symmetrically and relax her arms and shoulders, she could protect the vulnerable rib and row hard. The happiest result of her personal discoveries was that she learned to "de-intellectualize" her sculling. Her intuitive understanding has enabled her to become a fine sculler and a successful coach.

The Sculler at Ease

JOHN BIGLOW

My most vivid recollection of John Biglow is watching him on a bright day on Lake Washington rowing full-out, lifting the bow of his Pocock single with each stroke, keeping it running out over the water on each recovery, a glorious demonstration of power, speed and grace.

John Biglow began to learn the hard lessons of boat racing when he was a youngster at the Lakeside School in Seattle. On one notable occasion he demonstrated his generalship in a junior varsity four in the season's championship finale, held on Shawnigan Lake on Vancouver Island, British Columbia. From the shore we could see John's four struggling to stay with the competition through the early stages of the race. The outcome looked extremely doubtful. All at once the stroke rate dropped and the four broke away. They won easily. Afterward John approached me shouting, "It worked, it worked!" He then explained that, when things were going badly, he knew he had to do something, so he told the cox to drop the stroke. He encountered some resistance to this idea, but persisted and got the cox to command "Down four!" Of course, no one in the boat had ever heard such a command before, but willy-nilly, John stretched out the next recovery and the crew followed him down.

He had, like most of the great scullers and rowers, one small idiosyncrasy. In our efforts to eliminate every extraneous gesture from his sculling we were generally successful. We could agree that such movement was wasteful of energy. I insisted that even the appearance of effort was energy wasted, as for example, when he grimaced every time he set his sculls, I was convinced—I am still convinced—that grimacing begets tension just as much as it is the outward sign of tension. It was like telling a baseball pitcher not to pull at his cap, or spit, or to do one of a dozen things a pitcher finds to do before he throws the ball. John would try to hold his face still, but the habit was so ingrained that it cost him more effort not to set his

142

face than it did to grimace.

He represented the United States on five consecutive teams, was the fastest sculler in the country in 1981, 1982 and 1984, won at Henley stroking a four, took two bronzes in the single in consecutive World Championships in 1981 and 1982, and came fourth in the single in the 1984 Olympiad.

PAUL ENQUIST
In Greek legend Procrustes was a robber who offered hospitality to wayfarers. Once they were in his house, he forced them onto a bed which they had to fit or else have their limbs stretched or lopped off to measure. Probably the severest test I have faced as a coach is finding ways to accommodate extremes in the physical dimensions of athletes within the dimensions of conventional rowing equipment.

At 6'–7" Paul Enquist was the tallest athlete I have coached. He was so long in his arms and legs that we could not find equipment to accommodate him. If he positioned himself properly at the catch, he felt exactly as he should feel: that he was ready to shove the boat forward with a mighty thrust of his compressed legs. But in this position his long arms took the blades so close to the boat that he spent the first 20 degrees driving the water sideways. We couldn't move him forward in the boat because we couldn't extend his slide any farther. We had to settle for a shorter run down the slide. Even after he accepted the idea, he found it very difficult to restrict his movement. It felt very strange. One day we were out for a Sunday row, and for fun someone suggested that he row as high a rate as he could for a short burst. He broke 40 strokes per minute and magically began to move the boat and look good doing it. "But," he said, "I'm rowing a short slide." It was a good many months later that he accepted the drastic restriction in his use of the slide that allowed him to row within the most efficient arc, 85 degrees.

We got another hint of the kind of sculling he was capable of in a race, a scant mile sprint, in which Paul struggled to beat a stablemate of lesser potential, a man who, it seemed, could always muster enough speed to beat him. Just as Paul crossed the finish line, he rowed two beautiful strokes; all the strain and effort disappeared and he rowed with grace and ease—two strokes—and then lay on his oars. When he came ashore he asked me what I thought of his performance. I had to tell him the truth. I said, "The best strokes you rowed were the two strokes after you crossed the finish line." Later, he understood that he had accomplished something that, brief though it was, had up to that time seemed out of reach. In those two strokes, he sat up, didn't strain or force an undue curve in his back and gave himself the moment of relaxation before catching. Three years later, he put over 200 of those strokes together and with Brad Lewis rowed to a gold medal in Los Angeles.

SHERRI CASSUTO
Good rowers and scullers, like all accomplished athletes, put enormous importance on the way they feel the movements of their bodies. They depend on their muscle sense, their awareness of the relative position of various parts of their bodies. They are so tuned to nuances of feeling, that any change in the way they use their bodies may be experienced as discomfort. When they violate this intuitive knowledge, they experience discomfort and sometimes injury.

In 1984 Sherri Cassuto had earned a place in the national team eight when an injury in her neck caused her to lose feeling in her right arm. She went to the Los Angeles Olympiad as a spare. On her return she and I were in singles enjoying an easy row when I noticed that she was forcing a bend in her back that put an awkward kink in her neck as she tried to keep her head up. It turned out that she had adopted this posture at the urging of her coach. It seemed to me that there had to be a connection between her artificial posture and her injury. In fact, she had incurred some erosion of several spinal disks and had already undertaken a series of chiropractic treatments that she continued for the duration of her subsequent training. She readily agreed to abandon the bend in her back that I objected to.

Sherri again tried out for the national team in 1985 and with her partner Susan Broome rowed a pair to a silver medal in the World Championships. Using her body in the way that she knew was appropriate she was able to complete another strenuous campaign with no recurrence of her injury.

Early in August, 1987, after Sherri Cassuto had been selected as the single sculler on the U.S. national team, she met me for some coaching. Sculling alongside her, I noticed the same tendency to put her blades in the water with her wrists that I had seen in June before the trials for the team. When I set about correcting her, asking her to start the stroke with her legs and let her fingers curl in reaction as the blade intercepted the water, she became very apprehensive: how could she learn something "new" this close to her departure for Copenhagen? I suggested that she try anyway, and encouraged her to talk about the World Championships ahead. For the next half hour or so we jogged along, engrossed in conversation. I noticed an improvement in her catch. After a bit, I interrupted her to observe that she was doing very well. "Sure," she said, "but what will happen when I race?"

I erupted with a very emphatic discourse about the absolute necessity of preparing herself to race in world class competition by sparing no effort to perfect her technique. An operatic diva or a première danseuse, I said, would do no less to prepare for a command performance. But of course she was right. She was sure that under pressure she would lapse into habits acquired while rowing. It didn't matter, after all, that these changes were small, very easy to perform or guaranteed to add to her speed.

Following the World Championships, in which she came in sixth, Sherri remedied her hold and polished her sculling in preparation for the 1988 Olympic trials. She qualified for a seat in the quadruple sculls and represented the United States in Seoul.

An interesting footnote to Sherri's extraordinary record as a competitive athlete is that she settled on a professional career as a Rolfer. Buttressed by a thorough study of human anatomy, her considerable intuitive understanding is now serving a diverse clientele among whom are a number of local rowers and scullers.

PERSPECTIVES

BERT HAINES

At Harvard in 1940, rowing for Bert Haines, an English professional sculler who came to the U.S. after World War I, I heard for the first time of Steve Fairbairn. Although Haines evidently respected him, I had no clear idea of the similarity of their views until I read *Steve Fairbairn on Rowing.*

In particular, Haines and Fairbairn seemed to agree on the proper use of the back. They both advocated the method of taking the catch that carried over from the days of fixed-seat rowing. Fairbairn never mentions the possibility of injury to the back at the beginning of the stroke.

While I rowed at Harvard under Haines' tutelage I never heard of a back injury. Correct posture on the seat was the first thing Haines insisted on. He asked his oarsmen to sit as Fairbairn put it, *"...as far over on the flat of the hams as possible...."* I remember that this took effort, but as the deep loin muscles get stronger you are better able to keep your back from bellying out under the strain of beginning the stroke. In this way all the power of your legs plus the weight of your body is transferred to the oar, with the result that you rise off your seat. If you let your lower back bend you leave a large portion of your weight in the boat. Proper posture and the correct tension in the loins, both Haines and Fairbairn agree, make it impossible to hit your front stops.

Fairbairn was very emphatic about the hooped back: "Never coach to drive the back out, but to work the blade as far as possible." For Haines, too, the finish of the stroke was not some arbitrary distance in front of the body, but as far back as the handle could be carried. For the rower this means the thickness of a T-shirt from the body.

The sculler's handles just pass the plane of his stomach.

Good rowing and sculling depend on nice blade work. Both Haines and Fairbairn knew that the blade must begin its return while it is still under water. "Start turning the blade onto the feather just before flicking it into the air," says Fairbairn. Notice, he does not say, "Feather the blade." The blade assumes the feathered position as it leaves the water, heading toward the bow. "The beginning of the movement of getting the hands away is to start turning the blade on the feather just before the finish of the stroke." Haines insisted that we keep our puddles down. Haines taught us that the only way we could accomplish this was to turn the blade while it was under water, with a slight rocking of the wrist, a quarter turn. With the wrist held firm, the handle is thrust away. The wrist then straightens and the handle is rolled out under the second joint of the fingers. Fairbairn agrees: "Turn the blade with as little wrist work as possible, and especially, see that the wrist does not sag."

Fairbairn's coaching, like Haines', was directed whenever possible at the sensory rather than the intellectual perceptions of the rower. "Squeeze the button through the rowlock" overstated the point a bit, but the oarsman knew what he ought to feel. The secret of the turning of the blade at the end of the stroke is in maintaining lateral pressure to keep the collar pressed into the rowlocks, a virtual refrain in Haines' coaching.

A comparison of Haines and Fairbairn is illuminating because it points up the degree to which the masters of the sport understood not only the essence of safe and economical sculling and rowing, but also the most effective way to communicate their understanding. Although Fairbairn was a university man and Haines a tradesman, their preeminence as coaches and teachers followed from the wisdom they shared, that is, that skill in a boat depends upon the full play of the senses.

Bert, as he was called by all his oarsmen, and I were standing together on the Princeton dock at Lake Carnegie after the Eastern 150-pound Championships in 1942, waiting for the varsity race to come down the course.

"Dutch Schoch told me an interesting thing about your crew, Frank," said Bert. "He said, 'you could have put an egg on the end of every rigger of your JV boat and they would have gone up the course and come back down again without losing an egg.' " The ghost of a smile and the sparkle in his eye showed that he had enjoyed the compliment to his skill as a coach—relished it enough to want to pass it along to me. He made me feel as though I were being admitted to a guild of artisans.

Bert was first and last a craftsman. He could not tolerate torn water, the boil and foam off the blade that betrays poor technique. Nor large white puddles, nor missed catches, nor short finishes. He taught bladework as only a superb sculler understands it. He taught the use of the oar as a tool, with the craftsman's understanding that a good tool, well-designed for its use, will do its work supremely well if you let it. When he stopped a crew, he would begin at the bow and describe each man's performance in turn, giving him precise instructions for improvement. From bow to stroke he rarely repeated himself, since each man's rowing was clear and unique in his mind before he began. He could, as few coaches can, keep each oarsman "thinking actively," in Steve Fairbairn's phrase, about his own contribution to the boat.

He was adamant about keeping our eyes in the boat. There was work to be done and the only way to do it was to concentrate on it to the exclusion of every distraction, every sight and sound that didn't issue from the boat. We were taught to row our own race; the competition would fall behind us in good time. The first stroke of a racing start told the story. If the blades were hooked in solidly, there would follow a brief moment of suspended motion while the oars bent and the boat hesitated. Instantly thereafter, it shot away like an arrow from a bow.

He never made speeches. I remember once sitting at our oars and watching Bert approach us in his launch—white golfer's cap, white locker room towel around his neck, bulky sheepskin jacket nearly doubling his size, a cigarette protruding exactly from the center of his mouth. He spoke as always, around the cigarette. "Well, Frank," he said, "Your crew has two speeds: dead slow and stop." I think he had been saving that particular mot for just the right moment, for I never heard it again. He smiled his barely discernible smile, while we digested this judgment upon our well-meant but clumsy efforts. He relieved our chagrin that the best we could do only amused him, by going over our little lapses with just as much patience and just as much good humor as if he had already made up his mind that we were going to come as close to the ideal crew that existed in his head as any he had ever coached. And off we went again in pursuit of our own imperfect vision of the Holy Grail.

One member of the varsity crew told me that in his sophomore year, rowing in the varsity boat, he had become impatient with the rolling of the boat and sharply lifted his hands to yank his rigger up. Bert said not a word. But when the oarsman looked at the lineups posted in the tobacconist's window on Massachusetts Avenue next day, he found himself assigned to the JV boat. He finished the season there. He never asked Bert why he had been dropped from the varsity; Bert never told him. It would have been totally unnecessary. He had broken the cardinal rule: never express your feelings to the detriment of the crew.

Bert believed that if you tended to the work at hand with all the concentration and all the energy you had, you would be doing all you needed to do to win races. His thinking about the racing start and the starting sprint was to execute it as flawlessly as possible—and then get on with the race.

The key to this was the "settle," when the stroke came down and the rhythm and pace of the next five minutes were established. A crew that settled well raced well. The alternative, horrible to contemplate, was to scramble to the finish line. "Sprint if you like, ten strokes, well into the race, if you think you need to." We used to take our "Tens" out of sight of the other crews whenever possible, under the bridge on the Charles River Basin course. With devastating effect.

The day before my first race as stroke of the freshman lightweight crew, I asked him how I should conduct the race. He looked at me for a moment, smiled and said, "Just get ahead at the start and stay ahead—" and turned and walked away. It seemed to me at the moment that he might have been a little more helpful. Later it occurred to me that, from his point of view, he had already made it quite clear how races should be rowed—in day after day of practise. It was so obvious! One minute into the race the coxswain announced that we were a quarter of a length down. So much for Bert's offhand advice. Time to go to work, settle the crew and row our own race—which, in due course, we won handily.

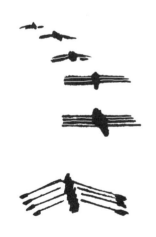

Bert was, as far as I could tell, unambitious. He had won enough races as a professional sculler and coach to know that we held our destinies in our own hands. He knew who he was and what he was. Our winning or losing was not going to alter that.

THE THAMES WATERMEN

*"If your Majesty will only tell me the right way to begin,
I'll do it as well as I can."*
Through the Looking Glass

In one essay of his book, *The Student as Nigger*,[5] Jerry Farber takes aim at the mentality that mars the educational process. The essay is entitled, "Teaching Johnny to Walk." It purports to be a pilot study directed at "the formulation of a viable theoretical basis for ambulation instruction on the normal pre-school level." For the purpose, forty normal children are to be taught how to walk by being first, "institutionalized and discouraged from all spontaneous and voluntary attempts at ambulation," and second, taken through a structured learning situation, "embracing ten phases of ambulation." Farber includes graphic representations of the ten ambulatory phases in stick figures, each identified by terse descriptive phrases in the best academic tradition: "dextral thrust-supra-patellar, sinistral monopedal suspension..." all in sequential order.

In brief, at the end of one year, the little ones have arrived at the seventh phase of ambulation; that is, they have completed one step with the left foot and they are now ready to learn how to put the right foot on the ground. In other words, the children have not yet learned how to walk.

The putative author of the study is not troubled by this apparent lack of progress, since he is more concerned that the children acquire "an intellectual command of their achievement," something he is sure cannot be said of children who are taught to walk by "folk methods". Lacking the ability to identify and name such concomitants of walking as "bounce, sway, inclination and more important, pelvic arc," how will they in their turn be able to teach their own children, "having themselves been trained in so intuitive and amorphous a fashion?" What, in fact, will they know?

All of which, I think you will agree, sounds ludicrous. But the sport of rowing has, I think, taken on a stitched-to-gether look because it is learned piecemeal, in just the same way as walking was learned by the children in Farber's satire.

It is hard to imagine that the Thames watermen who bequeathed us the sport of rowing went through anything like this experience. Quite the contrary. They learned at their oars, on the job, as apprentices. They were tool users and working men before they were athletes, that is before they contended for prizes. For them, the whole went before the parts; they learned intuitively and by example. Since these watermen had learned the art of rowing long before it became an amusement for gentlemen, they would seem to have been the logical source of instruction. Unfortunately, distinctions of class made that impossible. The professional oarsmen wrote no books. They had no coaches, as we understand the term, but instead the example and the accumulated wisdom of the men who rowed the fastest. What these men and others like them were able to pass along was a mastery of the oar that depended on the intuitive understanding of the use of a tool.

It wasn't merely inverse snobbery that made the old watermen take the writers of books about rowing lightly. They could, after all, observe the university men rowing. Occasionally, they met on the water in friendly competition. Not that they were permitted to enter gentlemen's regattas. But sometimes the winner of the prestigious Diamond Sculls would take up the challenge of the professional and, as a rule, lose. In short, the professional watermen had no reason to envy the amateurs.

Today's amateur rowers are in the very same predicament as the gentlemen of yesteryear, but for a different reason, more directly related to the outboard motor than to class distinction. They enter the sport for the most part in an academic setting, where coaches teach it like an academic subject. And they enter it quite without the skills that other athletes bring with them to their sports. I can't believe that anyone today turns out for a basketball team who hasn't tossed a basketball through a hoop, or dribbled one on any convenient slab of concrete.

Basketball great Larry Bird once was asked to act in a television commercial for a candy bar company. A little girl in the crowded stands of Boston Garden was supposed to crunch her candy bar so loudly that The Bird was distracted into missing a layup. What could be easier? Roll camera. Try as he might, he just couldn't miss the hoop. "Try aiming to the side of the net," they told him. Whoosh, right through. "Turn your back and just throw the thing." Whoosh again. He was simply incapable of missing the hoop. How did they get their picture? Trade secret. The Bird just wasn't programmed to fail.

Skills like his can't be taught. Get in a boat at every opportunity. Keep sculling until you discover what Robert Frost meant by "the pleasure of taking pains," or John Ciardi[6] when he wrote *"brilliance is the appetite for work not as drudgery but as joy."*

NOTES

[1] Menuhin, Yehudi. *Violin and Viola.* London: Macdonald and Company, 1976.

[2] Herbert, Marie. *The Snow People.* New York: G.P. Putnam and Sons, 1973.

[3] Fairbairn, Ian, editor. *Steve Fairbairn on Rowing.* London: Nicholas Kaye, Ltd, 1951.

[4] Herrigel, Eugen. *Zen In the Art of Archery.* New York: Vintage Books, a division of Random House, 1989.

[5] Farber, Jerry. *The Student as Nigger.* New York: Pocket Books, 1969.

[6] Ciardi, John. *Manner of Speaking.* New Jersey: Rutgers University Press, 1972.

GLOSSARY

AFT: (adjective) Sternward.

BACKSPLASH: Water pushed ahead of the blade prior to entry. "The latest freak thing" in Steve Fairbairn's phrase (1930) because it was being taught as a means to achieving a good catch. It becomes inevitable so long as the oarsman believes that the blade should enter the water before changing direction.

BACK STOPS: Small barriers on the track that arrest the motion of the seat in its progress toward the bow.

BLADEWORK: The way the blade is used to move the boat. Good bladework changes rowing from exercise to art.

BLIND BOAT: A boat which has no coxswain to steer it. Also called STRAIGHT, as in STRAIGHT FOUR or STRAIGHT PAIR.

BODY ANGLE: The angle of the torso to the horizontal, as regarded at the lower end of the spine.

BOW: from Danish *bov*, shoulder; from Old Norse *bogr*, shoulder. The front of a vessel.

CADENCE: The rate of the stroke.

CATCH: The entry of the blade, so-called because the blade has to overtake the water as it passes the boat.

CHECK: The interruption of the boat's progress caused by poor slide control or faulty blade work.

COAMING: probably from *comb* as the crest of a cock. Any raised structure around the cockpit of a boat. Also, SAXE-BOARD or WASHBOARD.

COLLAR: A stopper encircling the oar that prevents it from sliding through the rowlock.

COUNTERMOTION: Motion accompanying another motion in the opposite direction.

COXSWAIN: from Middle English *cokswayne, cok, cock,* a small boat, usually a tender to a larger vessel, plus *swayne, swain,* a servant akin to Old English herdsman. The person who tends or steers a small boat.

CRAB: from Middle English *kerven,* from Old English

ceorfan, to notch or carve. The crustacean so-called is noted for its ability to carve its way quickly into the sand. In the expression, CATCH A CRAB the word has been changed by folk etymology to a noun, and the meaning obscured. To carve the water unintentionally with the leading edge of the blade.

CREW: The complement of a boat. Not the name of the sport, a misunderstanding which has spawned the execrable phrase, "crew team."

DEAD SLIDE: Rowing without sliding up to the catch.

DECK: The cloth or plastic cover of the ends of the boat's hull.

DRAW: See PULL-THROUGH

DUMP(ING): The act of shoving the handle down to clear the blade from the water before the stroke has been completed.

ERGOMETER: A machine for measuring work and for exercising.

FEATHER: To trim the blade so as to offer the least resistance to the air on the recovery. It is accomplished by allowing the flat part of the loom to settle in the sill of the rowlock, pivoting the handle under the first joint of the fingers after the blade starts forward.

FIN: See SKEG

FOREWARD: Bow-ward from the middle of the boat.

FREEBOARD: The part of the hull above the water.

FRONT STOPS: Small barriers on the track that arrest the motion of the seat in its progress toward the stern.

GIRTH: The measure around the hull from gunwale to gunwale, a dimension related to the carrying capacity of a vessel.

GUNWALE (or GUNNEL): from Middle English *gunnewale.* The upper edge of the side of a small boat.

HORNS: The fore and aft supports of a seat that carry the wheels.

INBOARD: The measure of the oar from the tip of the

handle to the working face of the collar or button.

KEEL: Longitudinal beam running down the center of the boat on the outside.

KEELSON: Longitudinal beam running down the center of the boat on the inside.

LANE: The path intended for one and only one crew from the start to the finish of a race, marked by rows of small buoys within easy reach of the oar.

LEADING EDGE: The edge of the blade that parts the air or the water.

LEE: from the Old English *hleo*, covering, shelter.

LEEWARD: Away from the wind. The direction toward which the wind is blowing.

LEG DRIVE: The movement that places the entire weight of the body on the stretcher, and the blade of the oar in the water.

LOOM: from the Old Norse word *hlummr*, the handle of an oar. Now used to describe the entire shaft from the handle to the throat of the blade.

OAR (or SWEEP): Same implement as a scull but requiring the use of both hands.

OUTBOARD: The measure of the oar from the face of the collar to the tip of the blade.

OUTRIGGER: See RIGGER

OVERLAP: The crossing of the scull handles at midstroke.

PIN: see THOLE

PITCH: Upward and downward motion of the ends of the boat, very detrimental to speed. Also an angle, as between the rowlock face and the thole pin, between the blade and the face of the rowlock, between the rower's bench and the waterline, between the footboard and the gunwale.

PORT: from the Latin *portus*. Passage, door, haven, harbor, hence the harbor side of a vessel from the convention implicit in *larboard*, from the Middle English *ladeborde*, the side used to lade the ship.

PUDDLE: An eddy or disturbance left in the water by the blade at the end of the stroke.

PULL-THROUGH: The act of prying the boat past the blade.

RATE or CADENCE: Number of strokes per minute. Sometimes regarded as having magical properties as: the higher the rate, the greater the speed.

RATIO or PROPORTION: The relationship between the time taken to drive the boat forward and the time taken to bring the rower aft for the next stroke. Experience tells us that the latter should be greater than the former. The precise relationship has to be judged intuitively. When it is right, the boat seems to move without interruption; when it is wrong the boat lurches forward.

RECOVERY: The whole interval of time between the release and the catch.

RELEASE: The disengagement of the blade from the water, properly achieved by turning the blade underwater and beginning the "recovery" while the blade is buried. Not to be confused with the FEATHER.

RIGGER: Formerly OUTRIGGER, a frame to carry the thole or swivel farther from the keel than the gunwale to increase the usable length of the oar and its leverage.

RIGGER STAY: Any of several elements of the rigger.

RIGHT-OF-WAY: The right of one boat crew to proceed in water about to be occupied by another, a right taken for granted only by the foolhardy.

ROWLINE: A line perpendicular to the centerline of the boat passing across the working face of the rowlock.

ROWLOCK: A metal or plastic device that embraces the oar and swivels about the thole.

RUN: The progress of a boat between strokes.

SAXEBOARD: See COAMING.

SCULL: verb: To row a boat with two oars for each

rower. To make a figure eight underwater to push the boat sideways. noun: One of the pair of oars you scull (verb) with.

SHELL (RACING SHELL): formerly FINE or BEST BOAT. A boat used for racing. So called because of the thinness of the planking or skin.

SHIM: A wedge of metal, wood, plastic, or found materials placed between the hull and the rigger to raise or lower the rigger.

SKEG: from the Old Norse *skegg*, beard, or projection. A short keel or blade of metal or plastic. Necessary for directional stability.

SLEEVE: A protective plastic sheath secured to the loom of the oar where it passes though the rowlock.

SLIDE: The distance travelled by the seat during the stroke.

SPACING: The separation of puddles produced by the same blade in successive strokes.

STARBOARD: from the Old English *steor*, steering oar, plus *bord*, the side of a ship. The steering oar side, always the right side of a ship.

STATEROOM: The space allotted to each rower in a racing shell.

STEM: from the Old Norse *stamin*. The foremost part of a ship.

STERN: from the Middle English *sterne*, akin to the Old Norse *stjorn*, the act of steering. The aftermost part of a boat.

STRETCHER: from the Middle English *strecchen* , to extend. A short cross-beam that supports the feet in rowing.

STROKE: The sternmost rower in a team boat.

STROKE RATE: Cadence or beats in "strokes per minute."

SWEEP: see OAR

THOLE: from the Middle English *thole*, peg, from the Old English *thol*, peg. The projection from the side of an open boat against which the oar bears.

THWART: from the Middle English *thwert*, from the Old English *thweorth*. A transverse structural part of a boat.

TRACK: Two rails upon which the seat rolls.

TRAILING EDGE: The edge opposite the leading edge.

TRIM: The fore-and-aft attitude of a boat in the water. When it is correct the boat will perform at its best and ride on its designed optimum waterline.

WAKE: The track of a boat, an excellent aid to course-keeping.

WASHING OUT: Letting the blade rise out of the water before the end of the stroke.

WATERLINE: The line made on the hull of the boat where the surface of the water marks the equilibrium between the rower and his boat and the weight of water displaced.

WATERMANSHIP: The management of a boat with safety, skill and ease. The final test of a crew.

WAY: The progress of a boat through the water as in steerage way, lee way, under way, way enough.

WEIGH: No such thing in rowing (unless you're carrying an anchor).

WHERRY: from the Middle English *whery*. A long light rowboat originally used for transporting people.

WINDWARD: Direction from which the wind is blowing. To move to windward is to head into the wind.

WINNING: Not, as sometimes supposed, everything, but a short-lived state of affairs from which dreams are made and illusions fostered; one small step toward mastery.

INDEX

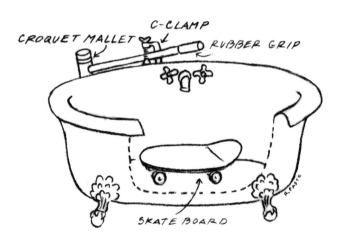

C-CLAMP

CROQUET MALLET

RUBBER GRIP

SKATE BOARD

....and practice, practice, practice.

SLIDING SEA

RISE.

RIB OR
SHOULDER.

THWART

KEELSON

TRACK

BOW

ROWER'S BEN

WHERRY